How to get PR for your Startup – Traction

By

Murray Newlands and Drew Hendricks

About the authors

Drew Hendricks contributes to a variety of different publications including Forbes, The Huffington Post, National Wildlife Federation, Technorati and many others on a variety of different topics. Drew is COO of AudienceBloom. Drew Hendricks is an experienced marketing professional and social media strategist with more than five years of experience in creating successful campaigns for clients. During this time, he has had the opportunity to work with clients in a wide variety of industries, from colleges and career schools to medical professionals. Drew serve as a freelance social media strategist, working with clients to craft innovative digital marketing campaigns that generate user activity and provide a high ROI. Through his social media marketing experience, Hendricks has gained a skill for devising social media strategies that result in a high conversion rate.

Murray Newlands LLB Solicitor FRSA contributes to Entrepreneur.com, Inc.com, and VentureBeat where he writes and produces videos on entrepreneurship, tech and social marketing trends and startup advice. His work has been featured on The Wall Street Journal, The Guardian, Forbes, The Huffington Post and many other publications. Newlands is a marketing and public relations professional, having founded several media firms. Newlands was Non-Executive Director for Slough Enterprise Hub and Cambridgeshire Business Services. He is on the advisory board for VigLink, the leading platform for content-driven commerce. Newlands received a Bachelor of Laws and he is qualified as a Lawyer. He gained his Green Card by being recognized by the US government as an "alien of extraordinary ability." Newlands is the author of "Online Marketing: A User's Manual" published by John Wiley and "Content Marketing Strategies for Professionals".

Foreword

Entrepreneurialism is skyrocketing, funding is readily available, and new ideas are flowing. Yet, today's startups face challenges unlike ever before; the crowded startup space leaves little room for the most important aspect of bringing any product to market: establishing awareness and credibility.

To many entrepreneurs, the old saying "It's not what you know, it's who you know" seems to ring more true than ever, especially when it comes to getting press coverage for their startup. CEOs and business owners are experts of their craft, but in many cases, have never had occasion to correspond with multiple media outlets in an effort to earn press coverage. Many learn–the hard way–the pitfalls of approaching journalists and editors at media outlets without a proper pitch or story, and how doing so can damage credibility before relationships even begin. Others don't know where to start, or who to contact for advice.

Most entrepreneurs know that press coverage from authoritative, trusted publishers not only builds awareness, but lends credibility to new brands. In today's crowded competitive startup space, this credibility and awareness is often the key to generating enough revenue to sustain a new business. And the opportunity to achieve entrepreneurial success shouldn't be limited to those who are lucky enough to have existing relationships with major media.

Every entrepreneur deserves a fair chance at success, and motivation, perseverance, and strategic knowledge should be the essential elements of it; not pre-existing relationships. Motivation and perseverance must come from within, but strategic knowledge can be learned and refined. We hope this guide provides that missing element for success; and enables entrepreneurs the fair chance at success through major media coverage that they deserve.

Jayson DeMers CEO, AudienceBloom

Table of Contents

Who is This Book For?

This guide was created with one specific goal in mind: to teach startups how to generate positive media coverage, spread brand awareness, and boost customer acquisition. For most startups, positive PR is a fundamental aspect of growth, and takes top priority second only to securing funding. If you're an early-stage startup looking to bolster your reputation and recognition within your niche, this guide is for you.

Why is PR Important?

Proving traction, or your ability to gain a strong foothold in your industry, is important whether you are backed by investors or using your own money to fund your startup.

If you are able to receive positive press, it signals investors that you can effectively communicate your story to which others will listen and share. A great story can carry your brand a long way.

Generating positive press proves that (1) you have a compelling story you can convey, (2) you, as an entrepreneur, possess the ability to connect with the press and convince them to support your brand, (3) the press thought your story was interesting enough for their audience to hear, and (4) you have improved your opportunity to attract customers from the press.

With the increasing number of new businesses and marketplace competition, brand recognition and customer loyalty is more important than ever before. Thanks to the Internet and the steady rise of eCommerce, modern consumers have unlimited options and unfettered access to goods and services from around the world. Choosing your brand over your competitor is simply a matter of buying from a brand they know and like.

Consumers are also becoming much more hesitant to make purchases and are constantly looking for the best deals they can find on the highest quality products around. Online shoppers are doing their research and relying on the suggestions or recommendations of other consumers when it comes to making purchases. This means trusting your brand and having a good reputation is vitally important, especially to small businesses. Thus, having great press and reviews on your company from reputable sources is an asset to your business that ultimately helps consumers make a final decision and choose to purchase from you.

In the Internet age, online shoppers have access to endless amounts of information. As a result, it's incredibly important that your company is viewed as the leading brand and authority in your niche. Consumers make choices to buy from brands they believe in and feel personally attached to. To create that sense of loyalty, you need exceptional PR to shine a light on your business.

It's up to you to create and tell the story of your startup. Laying the proper groundwork for positive PR is crucial to avoiding false, negative information disseminated by others. You don't want the reputation of your business in anyone's hands but your own.

The bigger your brand and the more well-known you are, the easier it is to take your business to the next level. Positive PR is a way to tell your story, grow your brand awareness, and gain a legion of loyal fans and customers.

Chapter One
Defining Public Relations

You were on the precipice of launching your first business. In fact, you were so excited that you thought it would prosper right after the ribbon cutting ceremony. But all of your dreams shattered when you realized that none of it materialized.

Imagine this scenario: You are inside your store, waiting for curious customers to come in, but they merely pass by without giving your place of business a second look.

Regardless, you keep convincing yourself that you did your homework:

- You covered the "basics of starting a business."
- You have a killer name for your business.
- You know you have an awesome product to sell.
- You have an idea of your target market.

What went wrong?

Enter public relations.

What is PR?

The practice of public relations (PR) dates back to the early 20th century. Essentially, PR allows a company to maximize its chances to receive free editorial coverage. It's a marketing practice that every startup needs for an opportunity to be mentioned in highly revered publications such as *TechCrunch* or *The New York Times*.

However, technological advances have changed the way PR is defined. According to the Public Relations Society of America, PR "is a strategic communication process that builds mutually beneficial relationships between organizations and their publics."

These days, PR is more than simply gaining publicity; it's about working on your reputation. It includes relationship building among industry influencers and engaging your target audience. The aim of businesses nowadays is not only to gain exposure — it's also to make people trust them.

But here's the question: How can you obtain that opportunity of garnering media coverage for your business, especially in today's volatile market?

The answer is an effective PR marketing campaign.

In relation to this, there are two basic ways companies can receive exposure through PR: press releases and company mentions.

According to publicity guru Bill Stoller, "a press release is a pseudo-news story, written in third person, that seeks to demonstrate to an editor or reporter the newsworthiness of a particular person, event, service or product."

Press releases are typically directed at members of the news media (hence the term *"press* release") for the purpose of announcing something newsworthy. Examples of a press release include:

- Company launches
- Funding announcements
- Milestones
- Acquisitions

Company mentions, on the other hand, are having your name mentioned or referred to in a relevant article — usually in a form of quoting what you've said at an event or written on your official website. This occurs when reporters are looking to industry thought leaders for perspective or opinions regarding a relevant subject matter.

Either way, both practices allow your business to get into the spotlight and be known to your target audience — the people you think would benefit from your business. The more people get to know you, your business, or the products and services you offer, the bigger your chances of reaching out to target customers.

However, it should be noted that advances in technology have re-shaped the definition of public relations. Once a marketing tactic, it's now deemed as a communication process wherein you build a form of trade to an industry influencer. It could be as simple as celebrity A endorsing your products to his fans in exchange for a one-year supply of your products.

PR can do far more than simply gain exposure for your company. It can also improve your business' reputation and relationships with your influencers (also known as endorsers), journalists or members of the news media, and even your potential and existing customers. This could come in handy and may be extremely beneficial, especially in today's unpredictable and ever-changing market.

Why Startups Need PR

The goal of public relations is for your company to receive free editorial coverage, whether in a newspaper, magazine, or on a website. In addition, businesses nowadays are hyped up about bringing their message out through various media.

Thousands (if not millions) of press releases are published on the Internet everyday. With this in mind, you need to find a way to make your business stand out from the rest. This is what makes PR so important and the reason it should be part of your marketing strategy.

Aside from making sure that your startup, including the products and services you offer, can address your target market's needs, you must also consider how you can bring your business into the spotlight. In fact, getting exposure for your brand must be your highest priority before launch since you've sacrificed time, money, and sleep for your business.

PR is an important part of any marketing strategy — especially in today's media-saturated culture. One of the best ways to advertise your business is through editorial coverage. This can improve your brand's bottom line, business relationship, and reputation. Not to mention, PR can help your company raise money or even be acquired.

But other than gaining exposure for your company, PR also enhances your reputation and standing in the industry regardless of the content you provide or products and services you offer. This enables you to influence the media, which can result in creating positive impressions about you and your brand, as well as gaining greater reach into your target market.

But why does your startup need PR?

For Public Communication

Compared to marketing that focuses on promoting your business' products and services, PR is all about communicating with the public. Getting your message across allows you to share relevant information to your target customers, the media, and industry influencers. The more they get to know your brand, the more likely they will trust you and your business.

For Reputation Management

Aside from promoting your business, PR also lets you build a positive public image for your company. When people only hear or read good things about your brand, you can gradually earn the public's trust. This is very important to note, since consumers will only choose products or hire services from someone they trust. Gaining your target market's trust will enable you to establish an ideal relationship with them, as well as with industry influencers and members of the media.

For Damage Control

PR is also helpful for damage control. For example, your competitor in the industry starts spreading unpleasant rumors about your business. Of course it will reach your potential and existing and customers, which can seriously damage your reputation — online and offline. Hence, you need PR to neutralize the situation, clear the air, and tell your customers the truth.

In today's world, where every business is trying to establish their reputation and stand out in the market through online media, it's imperative that you have a well-constructed PR plan for your business. Whether you provide content, products, or services, the business that can influence the media will win the trust of the people — just because consumers typically decide to purchase from brands they trust and are familiar with.

Tips for Keeps: Start building your public relations campaign and create a buzz around your business, even before you launch it.

In the remainder of this book, you'll learn the do's and don'ts of PR, how to develop and create a great story for your brand, effective ways to build relationships with industry influencers and journalists, and how to execute your PR strategy to meet your business' marketing goals.

Chapter Two

PR and the Internet

There is no denying that the Internet has changed the way people promote themselves. Nowadays, anyone can provide creative content and get the chance to be the next Internet sensation.

How many singers have you heard of who started their career by uploading videos on YouTube?

Meanwhile, the World Wide Web has opened doors of opportunities for businesses, most of which remain unavailable with traditional media. Many a restaurant owner has gained popularity through food blogs, while numerous fashion stylists started their career as a fashion blogger.

In relation to this, more and more Internet trends are arising, which businesses can take advantage of to drive PR campaigns on the Web.

Multi-media Content is in Demand

According to marketing specialist Fred Godlash, 65 percent of the world's population are visual learners, indicating that text-only content is becoming a thing of the past. Allow your audience to consume your content the way they like it by incorporating images and videos within your text. Better yet, repurpose your old but still-relevant (also known as "evergreen") content and turn it into an infographic, online PowerPoint presentation, or video tutorial.

"People are often confused by where to start with content. I always tell them to start by what they read on their industry: as a startup founder, you should do that anyway and if it doesn't feel easy and interesting, you're doing the wrong startup. So as you do that, you will very naturally be able to curate the good stuff from the average one and chances are you'll have something to say about it: don't waste that reaction by keeping it to yourself but use it to create a curated post linking back to the original story you found interesting. As an entrepreneur in that industry, you have expertise and it matters: curating and publishing your reactions to good stories is a great way not only to bootstrap your content strategy but also to get noticed by influencers and media which cover that space. And by reading what others are writing, in no time, you'll also be coming up with good original stories very naturally: they'll be the ones no one has written yet."

Guillaume Decugis, CEO & Co-Founder at Scoop.it

Social Media Still Brings in Traffic Referrals

According to Mary Meeker's 2014 Internet Trends, social media traffic referrals will continue to grow. In fact, sharing cycle of articles on Twitter and Facebook lasts an average of 6.5 hours and 9 hours respectively. Buzzfeed content remains the most shared on Facebook, while BBC reigns on Twitter.

Do you want to take advantage of that sharing cycle and make the buzz around your recent blog post last for a couple of hours? Do not only share them on Facebook or Twitter — check out what these aforementioned websites publish, how they share it on their social media channels, and see if you can adapt their style for your press release.

Mobile Internet is Here to Stay

The Mary Meeker's study also states that mobile data traffic is increasing to 81 percent, with video consumption as the biggest use of mobile data. In addition, mobile ad growth is deemed to provide a $30 billion opportunity in 2014.

Such growth reveals that news consumption is not just moving online but also going mobile. Take advantage of the traffic that mobile Internet users can bring by making your website responsive. You can also add video clips on your online news coverage.

Re-imagining User Interface is the Next Big Thing

With the advent of social media and responsive web design, more and more online publications have embraced Web 2.0 to cater to their audience's needs. This is to prevent a decrease in traffic, as today's Internet users are willing to leave a particular website for its competitors due to bad user interface.

What does this mean for your business? Create a company website with streamlined design and incorporate social media so visitors can share your content easily. The more user-friendly your website is, the more user interaction it will experience.

Multi-media Sharing Shows Rapid Growth

Online users are not only creating and providing their own content; they also share third-party and relevant information to an audience. In relation to this, more tools are being created to increase peer-to-peer communication — making word-of-mouth recommendations more important than ever. Are you providing compelling and relevant content that your audience can share with their friends and family?

Start Writing For Your Audience

The 2014 Internet Trends state that 13 zeta bytes of content will be created and consumed this year. Therefore, it will be a significant challenge for your content to stand out from the noise. The best way to rise above the rest and encourage action is to write for your core audience.

With people all over the world going online to search for information, purchase products, and hire services, it's a no-brainer that the Internet plays an important role in shaping the public opinion. Therefore, a PR campaign that does not communicate a brand's message effectively online will have a difficult time shaping and maintaining a company's desired public image.

The Challenges of Internet PR

The Internet may have brought new opportunities for businesses to promote their products and services, but it has also created a number of challenges — especially for the PR professionals who have mastered the art of communication in traditional media.

Nowadays, everyone has the ability to share their opinion about everything to the entire world within seconds. The Internet has given its users the ability to reach millions of people with just a couple of clicks. There is no denying that the birth of the World Wide Web has provided PR pros with a powerful tool, but it has also forced them to compete against the entire world.

Imagine your business' competitors spreading rumors about your products and services on the Internet. Whatever malicious messages they publish on the Web will definitely smear your company's reputation, and your PR agent will have a hard time cleaning up the mess — making their job more difficult.

To prevent such hassle, you will need to be aware of the challenges a PR pro faces whenever they incorporate Internet to a campaign. Armed with such information, you can plan ahead and assist your business' PR efforts by mitigating any potential obstacles that may prevent a smooth transition into Internet-based marketing.

Chapter Three:
State of PR in 2014

It's said that online marketing is changing the way businesses do PR. However, PR professionals and specialists are simply incorporating the Internet into the mix to generate buzz, create earned media, and drive brand awareness.

In relation to this, the team behind Vocus®, a cloud-based PR and marketing software company, collaborated with Market Connections and launched The State of Public Relations 2014 last June. According to the report:

- Virtually every PR professional is responsible for all or some of their brand's "owned" content, while 53 percent of them use branded content in their outreach campaigns.

- The same number of practitioners use content marketing, and even fewer add search engine marketing to the mix.

- PRs with mobile engagement strategy are at 34 percent.

- In terms of ROI, 21 percent of PR pros use it as a key metric.

- Among the top five marketing and PR priorities, 54 percent focused on increasing brand awareness, while their biggest challenge was lack of staff or time and budget, at 51 percent and 48 percent respectively.

- Fifty-eight percent of public relations still identifies media as a successful distribution channel for interacting with customers, although it ranks behind websites (62 percent), email (60 percent), social media (60 percent), and events (59 percent).

- Fifty-three percent of PR professionals use content marketing, while 49 percent use search engine marketing.

- Only 34 percent of PR practitioners have a mobile engagement strategy.

- Return-on-Investment (ROI) is a key metric for 21 percent of PR pros.

- The top 5 marketing and PR priorities are as follows:

  - Increase brand awareness (54 percent)
  - Content marketing (37 percent)
  - Social media marketing (36 percent)
  - Sales conversion (35 percent)
  - Generating leads (34 percent)

- Top marketing and PR challenges are as follows:

  - Lack of staff/time (51 percent)

- o Budget (48 percent)
  - o Measuring or demonstrating results (42 percent)
  - o Generating quality leads (31 percent)
  - o Driving website traffic (30 percent)
  - o Nurturing and converting leads (30 percent)

- The successful distributions channels are as follows:

  - o Websites (62 percent)
  - o Email (60 percent)
  - o Social Media (60 percent)
  - o Events (59 percent)
  - o Media (58 percent)

- Fifty-eight percent of PR professionals cite media as a successful distribution channel.

With the help of Vocus® and Market Connections' report, you can gain a general insight as to where PR is heading. Plus, it gives you an idea of other mediums to employ in your own marketing campaign as well as the hurdles you may need to overcome.

Chapter Four:
The Dos and Don'ts of PR

At this point, you are probably thinking that public relations is an effective way to promote your business and generate the exposure it deserves. After all, it's a venture that you have spent sleepless nights brainstorming and fervently working on.

However, there are aspects that journalists label as "bad PR" and "good PR." To keep your pitch from getting tossed aside by the pros, learn the dos and don'ts of PR.

DO Build Positive Relationships

As previously mentioned, PR is more than merely gaining exposure for your company. It's also about building relationships with the public. Throughout this guide, you will learn the importance of positive relationships with your potential customers, media professionals, and industry influencers, along with how to connect with your network.

DON'T Get Ahead of Yourself

Counting chicks before the eggs hatch is a no-no in PR. You have to keep in mind that it's a startup for which you are trying to garner exposure. Some influencers may decide to shed some light on your business, while others may not – the latter of which can be very disappointing. To give your business the best possible opportunities, you need to know how to create an effective PR strategy.

DO be prepared for the long haul

PR is a marathon not a sprint. You need to be wiling to invest time to nurture relationships with key influencers in your industry. Most likely it will not happen overnight. If you follow the tips and tricks outlined in this book you can succeed. The old adage is true here: 'The harder (and smarter) you work, the luckier you will get'

DON'T think PR is akin to being a 'one hit wonder'

After you identify influencers don't expect that one pitch will be all that is required to automatically win someone over. Says digital marketing expert Anita Newton 'a one and done approach to PR is akin to asking to negotiate salary after the first job interview.' Like any relationship, nurturing your PR contacts takes time and effort. But as you will see from the chaptes below, if done well the results can be incredible.

DO Prepare to Tell a Good Story

PR is a communication process. But it's not just about telling what your company can do for your market. It's all about making your business feel and look human by telling a good story. And there is no better person who can tell your company's story than you.

DON'T Be Explicitly Salesy

The role of PR is for your business to have an opportunity to receive editorial coverage — not to generate sales. While one way to perfect your marketing pitch is to reiterate how your products and services can respond to the needs of your target market, you should avoid giving off that annoying "you need to buy my product" vibe.

Chapter Five:
Start With Yourself — Getting
Started With PR

If you are someone who gets easily excited about launching a new business, chances are you might have overlooked your public relations campaign. That's okay. Getting started with your PR does not need to be external and expensive. In fact, the tools you need to kick off your campaign are within your business.

Products and Services

In the business world, your products and services are the reason your customers will come and will also be their reason to stay. However, the PR industry requires that you know your business well, as this is what the professionals must communicate to the public.

To create an effective PR campaign, you need to have a clear idea of what your products and services are all about. It should answer the following questions:

What can your target customers get from your products and services?

Instead of just stating your company sells eco-friendly air conditioning units with plasma filters, why not explain what consumers can get from it?

State that you provide eco-friendly ACs with plasma filters that can filter bacteria and viruses, which therefore produces cleaner and healthier air that lessens suffering from dust allergies or hay fever.

Simply put, you do not just sell AC units to keep the air cool; your product alleviates human health conditions, offering further benefits to the customer.

How would you describe your products and services?

Aside from the purpose, you should also be able to describe your products and services. Using our previous example, determine whether your eco-friendly ACs come in various shapes, sizes, and colors. What are its functions (other than keeping the air cool)? Can it also serve as a heater during winter? Do your AC units come with a silver ion filter that helps effectively eliminate bacteria in the air? What are your product's other benefits, and which of those are more likely an effect of plasma filters producing clean and healthy air?

How can you deliver your products and services to your customers?

It's also important to identify whether your customers can buy it in your store, in any other store, or online. Also consider how they can hire your services or bring your products home. Can they put it in a car compartment? Do you allow home delivery with free installation? If not, what are your alternative services?

The key here is to make the delivery process as convenient as possible for your customers. Your customers are more likely to stick by your side if your products and services make their lives easy. Otherwise, they will search for another company that offers the same — if not better — products or services.

How much does it cost and what buying conditions do you allow?

While affordability is most likely based on a customer's purchasing capability, you should be able to justify why your products and services carry their determined price tag. In addition, you should also keep in mind the buying conditions (cash, credit card, installment, check, cash on delivery, requires 50 percent down payment, etc.) of your potential customers. This is to allow your target customers to purchase your products or services with ease.

Knowing the answers to the aforementioned questions allows you to clearly communicate what your business can offer. Getting the right message out to industry influencers and PR pros allows them to bring your business to your target market's attention effectively.

Website

Having a company website is a great starting point to conduct an effective PR campaign, especially if you would like to take advantage of the numerous opportunities the Internet can offer. This is what allows you to connect to the world 24/7, not to mention that it can do wonders for your business' visibility.

A website serves as a digital home for all of your resources, making it accessible to the public.

When someone would like to know how to contact you, all they need to do is check out your website.

Have you recently launched a new product? Your customers can get the information straight from your website.

A distressed customer needs help troubleshooting. A customer support number can be found on your website.

The bottom line here is to make all necessary information available at your customers' fingertips.

Above all, don't forget to include a press page. Says Anita Newton, Digital Marketing expert "Journalists are incredibly resource constrained. Take the extra step and make it as easy as possible for them. Include product shots, lifestyle images, logos, news alerts, anything that can save them time.

In addition, a well-designed website makes a positive impression. A website's design can make a difference as to whether or not people choose to do business with you. As Steve Krug, author of *Don't Make Me Think*, puts it:

"[If] the people who built the site didn't care enough to make things obvious — and easy — [it] can erode our confidence in the site and the organization behind it."

Hence, beyond merely having a website, your digital home on the World Wide Web must allow you to convey the right message to your audience by providing accessible information regarding your business and the solutions it offers your potential and existing customers.

Content

Your content allows you to tell your company's story before everyone else does. In relation to this, a creative and well-crafted story gives your business a face, therefore making it human.

So, what can you do with your content to help boost your PR campaign?

Focus on Producing Creative Content

PR pros and specialists spend days working on press releases, compiling a list of target audiences and influencers, and writing pitches that explain why your business' story is newsworthy.

According to Amie Marse, founder of Content Equals Money, "Creative, unique, and compelling content is crucial to emblazoning your brand in the minds of consumers. With such stiff competition among businesses today, startups cannot afford to remain silent or unheard with respect to maintaining the voice of their business and industry. Well-written and relevant content is key to staying ahead of the competition."

Why not put that same amount of time and energy in crafting creative content? Construct something that your target audience will find useful, interesting, or even funny! It can be in a form of a blog post, video, slide show, infographic, or cartoon, as these are the types of content your readers would want to see or watch online. Unique, creative content will allow you to remain in the forefront of you reader's minds, now and in the future.

Inform Your Friends

The difference between informing your friends and writing your marketing pitch is in the story you share.

Using our previous example of air conditioning units with plasma filters, you can inform your friends on Facebook that you have created an infographic about the benefits of plasma filters. That's it. Pitching, on the other hand, explains to your friends why the infographic is so cool.

Bottom line: Make your content available in various online channels, and let your friends decide whether it's cool or not.

Let Your Content Do Its Work

One reason marketing campaigns fail is because professionals create a story about something that is not newsworthy. Instead of making the same mistake, think of something newsworthy and let the news spread on its own.

In conclusion, consider content as a tool to help describe your business' culture and what makes your brand special. Highlight the areas of your company, as well as the products and services you offer for which you want to be known.

Creating Something Newsworthy

As much as PR is about connecting with the right individuals and gaining access to avenues of exposure, it's also largely centered on a company's ability to develop and produce newsworthy content. Can you create something that is truly engaging and valuable to your audience? That's the major question regarding the creation of newsworthy content.

What Constitutes "Newsworthy?"

While the definition of news is "new information or a report about something that has happened recently," what makes something newsworthy? What takes a piece of news from simple text on a page to engaging content worthy of being reported and distributed? Those are the questions behind the idea of what constitutes newsworthiness.

While everyone has their own specific criteria that an event, incident, or happening must meet to be considered newsworthy, there are a few generally accepted rules. Newsworthy content must be timely, significant, interesting, and people-centric.

- **Timely.** Newsworthy content must be "new!" Companies often get it wrong from the start by thinking something is newsworthy even when it's old and recycled. For something to be newsworthy, it must be timely. For example, an engaging report about the death of a Civil War general may be interesting, but it's certainly not timely. For this topic to be newsworthy, it would need a timely tie-in with a current event or happening, such as the recent discovery of an artifact that explained previously unknown events regarding the general's passing.

- **Significant.** While timeliness is important, it certainly isn't everything. A story can be timely, but it lacks value unless it's significant to the audience. In the case of the Civil War example, the story may be newsworthy if the audience is from the same hometown as the general, or the discovery of the artifact will have a significant impact on the future of the area.

- **Interesting.** Does anyone care about the story? A timely and significant story that nobody cares about hardly constitutes a newsworthy story. There needs to be some part of it that is stimulating, engaging, or fascinating.

- **People-Centric.** If you take a look at recent news, you will notice one thing: every story is focused on people. Human interest is a must when developing newsworthy content. Regardless of what the story is about, it needs to tie back to people. How does it/will it/could it affect people?

Finding Newsworthy Content

Along with a proper understanding of what newsworthy content is, it's important to know how and where to find such content. Depending on the type of company or entity you are, the process can vary greatly. Companies often find newsworthy content in one of the following places:

- **Industry Sources.** Every industry typically has trade publications, content aggregation sites, or similar sources where industry-specific information can be found. Newsworthy content can often be discovered by browsing these sources.

- **Internal Developments.** Anything your company does that has an effect on customers or the general public may be newsworthy. This could include things like a new product launch, marketing promotion, or rewards program. Again, it will have to meet the "newsworthy" criteria, but valuable information can often be found internally.

- **Customers.** Customers and clients often make the best stories. They appeal to the human interest aspect and are often significant to your audience. If you have a customer or client that's found a particular use for your product or service beyond what it was designed to do, you may have a story.

Leveraging Newsworthy Content

Leveraging newsworthy content is all about understanding how your audience responds and where you choose to distribute and share news. Here are a few ways to get the most out of newsworthy content:

- **Draw Readers In.** Your newsworthy content should draw readers in. Where is it you want readers to go, and how do you want them to respond? If you want them to visit your website, blog, or product pages, is your newsworthy content funneling readers to that point? Properly leveraged news will encourage the reader to learn more elsewhere.

- **Engage With Readers.** Newsworthy content can only be utilized to its full potential when it engages with the audience in a tangible way. You can engage via comments, social media, or any number of other avenues. This takes your newsworthy story from merely a story to a chance to interact with the audience.

- **Finding Valuable Distribution.** If you truly want to leverage your newsworthy content, it's crucial to find valuable and efficient distribution channels. This allows you to reach the right audience and make the most out of your efforts.

Distributing Newsworthy Content

Valuable distribution channels for newsworthy content include social media sites, blogs, and press releases. Social media sites are particularly useful for their timely nature. Content pushed through these channels is consumed quickly — which capitalizes on the timeliness of the story.

Blogs are a good distribution channel because they are almost always directly connected with a company's website or online home. Content found here is easily recognized and credited to the authoring company.

Press releases are another great avenue for distributing newsworthy content. These releases come with great credibility and authority. Additionally, it's easy to get these out to your audience. Sites are always looking for press releases and will happily distribute them.

Benefits of Newsworthy Content

As you can see, creating something newsworthy is an extremely valuable and efficient use of time. When properly leveraged, it can provide the following benefits:

- **Credibility.** Newsworthy content enables you to appear as an authoritative and knowledgeable figure in your industry or corporate circle. By continually creating and distributing credible, newsworthy content, you will establish yourself as a worthy thought leader.

- **Traffic.** It's no surprise that newsworthy content drives traffic to your online pages. When the audience enjoys what they read, they will likely be interested in learning more from the source.

- **Exposure.** If you create something newsworthy, other sources and content aggregation sites may be interested in picking up your story. This leads to free exposure and advertising.

Getting publicity for your business is one of the biggest challenges you'll face when starting up. Journalists and PR specialists get hundreds of thousands of pitches every week. That's why you need to think outside the box to stand out and get the promotion that you want.

What Is Your Story? How To Position Yourself and Your Message

What real world need or desire are you meeting? Lyft gets from point A to B without using taxis — it fixes the broken transportation problem. Tinder enables straight people to hook up. Grinder enables gay people to hook up. Waze fixes the problem of getting caught in traffic and wasting time and reducing stress. LinkedIn enables users to network professionally. You need to boil down your startup to what it fixes and for whom.

When developing the story of your brand, you should first think about what you want to be known for and what problem are you solving. This will be an evolving journey as your company and its products or services change. But even if your company doesn't change, the world does not stand still around you and your message will need to evolve alongside it. The customers you target today might not be those you target tomorrow.

How does this look for a new company? It might mean targeting lower level people in smaller companies with a simpler message about usage, eventually evolving into persuading fortune 500 companies and governments to use your brand. This might happen by simply stating your opinion on a topic and eventually producing leadership pieces about the future of the industry or finding other means of becoming a thought leader or innovator in your particular niche. Try to think long term — make sure your brand will carry weight in 5, 10, 20 years, etc. Once you create your overall message, try to run it by your peers and potential users to see how well it works.

Review your competition and how they have built their brands. Reflect on and reconsider your own messaging and strategy.

It's always a good idea to remain proactive in creating and telling your story first, before anybody else has the chance to. First, outline your vision, where you see your place in the market, and what the general essence of your brand is. Think critically about this process, as you will be living with this story for the foreseeable future, and it must be genuine, unique, and appropriate for PR pros and consumers alike to trust it.

So how can you get started with your PR campaign? You must have the following:

Product

Your product is the starting point of your PR campaign. For journalists, PR specialists, and even your target market to check you out, you need to have something to sell. After all, the reason behind your campaign is to bring your product to your target customers' attention.

Service

Aside from products, you can also offer services or skills that you can render to other people to lessen your target customers' required workload. It's also one reason for PR professionals to check in on what you can offer. However, you must concentrate on the uniqueness of your business to stand out from the crowd. Otherwise, *you'll be that other company that offers such and such products and services.*

Website

With the boost the Internet can bring to your PR campaign, it's imperative that you include online marketing in your promotional efforts. For this to be effective, you need to have a website.

According to marketing communications expert, Riavon, your website represents you to the whole world, 24/7. That's why more than being well-designed, it should be able to get your message across accurately, as it can make a difference on whether people will choose to do business with you.

Content

Content allows you to create your story before somebody else does. Consider it a tool that can help describe your business culture and what makes your brand special.

Well-crafted content gives your company a face and makes it human by sharing the who, what, when, where, and why of your brand. To make it work, you need to create content (a blog post for example) that highlights the areas of your brand or products for which you want to be known.

How to Come Up With New Pitches

PR success very much depends on execution and quality of results. However, before anything can be executed or returns calculated, it's important to build a strong foundation. This strong foundation is sometimes difficult and time consuming to build, but when done properly, ensures success down the road.

The Value of the Pitch

What is the cornerstone of a strong foundation? The answer is a creative, well-developed, precisely defined pitch. A high quality pitch allows you to show your passion and commitment. It enables you to prove:

- **Preparation.** A good pitch requires considerable preparation and research. People can tell the difference between quickly thrown together pitches and those that took time to develop. If done correctly, your idea will prove you understand the topic, company, and audience enough to produce high quality results.

- **Focus.** A pitch will show how focused you are. This can either be good or bad, depending on what your company is looking for. If your pitch hits the mark, it will increase confidence in your idea. If poorly-developed and rushed, your pitch may come off as unorganized, lackadaisical, and too broad.

- **Success.** Ultimately, everything comes down to results. If your pitch proves there will be some benefit to the company's bottom line, it will almost always be approved.

The Mistake of Ignoring the Pitch

Unfortunately, many companies don't put enough focus into pitching. This is a dangerous road to travel and often ends up costing you in the future. It cannot be stressed enough: don't ignore the pitch! While you may be able to live off business connections and previous clients for a period of time, your lack of producing quality pitches will eventually hurt your business as competitors outshine you. Your company will slowly fade away.

Coming Up With New Pitch Ideas

Everyone is different, but for some, coming up with pitch ideas is the most difficult part of promoting a brand. Here are some tips to help you develop effective, high quality pitches every time:

- **Think Inside the Box.** You read that right; sometimes thinking inside the box can produce the best pitch ideas. People often get so caught up with thinking outside the normal parameters that they miss the easy ideas. Simple tried-and-true ideas can be the most effective. Has your company hired a notable executive recently? Is a new product release right around the corner? Why was last quarter so successful? Don't miss what's right in front of you.

- **Spin it a New Way.** Do you ever wish you had waited to pitch a story or idea? Often, you can get too anxious or ambitious and pitch an idea before it's fully developed. While you may have wasted that pitch, who's to say you can't put a fresh spin on an old idea? Take old, discarded pitches that you still believe in and look at them from a new, relevant angle.

- **Ask Around.** There is no weakness in asking for help. While the responsibility of developing and delivering a pitch may be in your hands, it's always okay to ask around for ideas. Talk to friends, family, and mentors. Different perspectives will yield new ideas.

- **Be Bold.** Are you too conservative with your pitches? Bold ideas are scary to deliver, but can be wildly successful in certain situations. Continually taking a conservative approach may bring slow, steady success, but is any ground really being made?

Fine-Tuning Pitches

Once you have developed an initial idea or train of thought, it's important to put it on paper and work out the kinks and issues. Even the best ideas need to be fine-tuned, and a failure to do so could result in a rushed pitch or half-completed thoughts.

The Big Three: Questions You Must Ask Yourself

In the PR industry, professionals often struggle with whether or not a pitch is good enough to be delivered. Just because you've spent time developing a pitch doesn't mean it's good enough to work. Save yourself time and embarrassment by asking these three major questions about every pitch you create:

- **Is it Interesting?** Above all else, the idea must be interesting. If the audience is not attracted to it, it doesn't matter if the pitch is relevant or serves the company's best interests. A topic or idea may be interesting internally, but does it provide excitement and engagement from an external point of view? If it checks off as interesting, proceed to question number two.

- **Is it Relevant?** There is a difference between interesting and relevant. You may find it interesting that local weather patterns have driven up industry demand over the past month, but is that relevant to your customers overseas? A pitch idea must be both interesting and relevant.

- **Does it Serve Our Interests?** It's compelling and relevant, but does it serve your best interests? You want to be honest with customers, but you also want to push out content and material that ultimately benefits your company. If something is interesting and relevant, yet may hurt your image, is it really worth putting out there? Probably not. Every pitch should be fine-tuned to make sure it serves the best interests of your company, while still remaining captivating and relevant to the target audience.

Delivering New Pitches

After preparations are complete, it's time to deliver your hard work and prove your pitch is indeed valuable and worth pursuing. Here are some good tips for effectively delivering a well-developed pitch:

- **Develop Rapport.** Much of your success will depend on the rapport you have with your audience. Whether you have an ongoing relationship with the individuals you are pitching to, or have never met them before, it's important to develop some type of working relationship. This often happens over time; other times it must occur within the few minutes leading up to the pitch delivery. During this period, prove you are friendly, professional, engaged, and interested.

- **Interact and Engage.** Nobody likes to be bored by a long-winded, pre-canned presentation. By interacting and engaging with your audience throughout the pitch, you will bring your idea to life.

- **Paint a Picture.** The best pitches are those that tell a clear story. A dull, clinical approach may cover your bases, but probably won't do your pitch justice. Paint a picture of what your pitch will say, how the audience will respond, and what the benefit will be.

- **Make it Natural.** You almost certainly practice pitches prior to delivery, but let things flow naturally. A scripted pitch just shows you are able to memorize well. A natural flowing pitch proves you are informed, engaged, and believe in the idea.

Creating new pitches is challenging and time consuming. While it can be tempting to overlook the value of the pitch and automatically start focusing on the next steps, it's important to build from the bottom up. A strong foundation with a well-developed pitch as the cornerstone will almost always lead to success.

You have to bear in mind that thousands, if not millions, of marketing pitches are being sent out to various PR pros. Instead of thinking how they can help promote your brand, find ways in which you, your business, or product can stand out from the rest. In return, it will prompt the specialists to help you gain that publicity you're looking for.

How to Construct Content

There are no hard and fast rules to this, but there are patterns from which we can learn.

Practical Content. Practical, useful content gets shared a lot. Case studies from within your industry are excellent if you can add some insight or an interesting twist to the story. "How to" posts about a current industry challenge or classic beginner issues are often not only set up to go viral, but are popular over the long-term as evergreen content.

News. If you can set up your publishing and social media team to be agile and informed, creating content around hot and trending news stories is a great way to bridge the gap between your target audience and the masses. Unless you are breaking that news, you should try to put your own angle on it to provide insight and make it relevant to your specific following. If you take time to plan, linking your content to an ongoing mainstream story can help generate months of viral traffic. For example, Kimling Lam and the Meltwater Group did an Election Buzz series linking social media analysis and the 2012 presidential election that brought them tens of thousands of YouTube views overall and was a great play for that crossover audience.

Seasonal. At certain times of the year, there are events that capture the attention of both the news and the public, and those are perfect opportunities for generating unique and timely content. For example, each Christmas, First Round Capital produces a Christmas video that always generates views and garners media coverage. This one has over 100,000 views. The great thing about these videos is that they feature the start-ups they invest in and give them exposure to a larger network, helping them gain new followers and new potential sources of site traffic and earned media sources.

Ride Trends. Current events and popular memes allow you to engage crossover audiences. For example, when Oreo came out to support gay rights, they hit the news, gleaning all kinds of media attention. While they may have lost some supporters as a result, they also received plenty of media coverage, helping them gain a legion of new fans. Not only did they take a stand on an issue, they also created a multi-colored cookie that worked well as an image on social media.

Bizarre. Find a quirky story that no one else has thought of, something that's intriguing enough to catch peoples' attention. Local media carry these types of stories all of the time. If you can't find a bizarre story to report, try to take a different angle on an existing story. The trick is to be creative and unique. For example, headlines like, "Customer uses super glue to save baby's life" or "Reader uses iPhone to build house" work as well in the local news human interest section as they do with online content.

Debates. Post about or comment on a conflict between people or a clash of ideas. People are always interested in reading about or watching drama unfold, so reporting conflicts is a great way to engage people and drive traffic. It's also a type of content that people are ready and willing to share, which will help get your content into networks of people outside your own. You don't necessarily need to inject your opinion into the conflict. You can just as easily discuss each side and talk about the implications of potential decisions and futures on your industry.

Statistics. People love numbers, and numbers make great headlines. Things like "A survey of 10,000 Microsoft Office users said that 97 percent love gray buttons" make for really engaging pieces. There are companies dedicated to creating surveys and PR specialists that focus solely on taking that data to market for you to create news.

Visual Content

Anytime you can create or integrate a video (interview, webinar, behind the scenes out-takes) or image (photo, infographic, Slideshare presentation) into your content strategy, you are increasing your viral potential. Networks like YouTube, Instagram, Pinterest, Facebook, and Tumblr are all social networks tailored around this kind of content where text plays a supporting role.

Lists. Lists are more of a format, but worth singling out as a popular type. They lend themselves to viral titles and social media descriptions, are super-easy for people to read, and allow you the freedom to root your own opinion and angle in a list that people can agree on. They are inherently optimized for easy skimming. They also let you highlight various points (and potential emotional triggers) in the same article.

Solve Problems. Do research in your field and see what people are struggling with. If you can create a piece of content that addresses and/or solves that problem, you've got a great piece of content on your hands.

Variety. These are types of content that you can mix and match. You can combine them for greater effect. Write a blog post with an infographic in it. Post an image with a quote on it. Make a video that outlines case studies. You get the idea.

Content Quality

Viral content from brands needs to be high quality and rock solid. It should reflect your brand and have a specific purpose, such as thought leadership, lead generation, etc. It needs to look and sound good.

Sure, low budget and iPhone videos go viral. Yes, the home page of Reddit's littered with viral animated GIFs about cats and Ryan Gosling. Blog posts and Facebook posts that look like chain letters regularly make their rounds online. That content is almost always personal or spammy content that goes viral organically.

Startups and even established brands can learn from those examples without falling into the trap of imitating them. For example, the Old Spice guy is in some ways a polished brand equivalent of the Ryan Gosling "Hey, Girl..." meme.

Branded videos, images, and text are going to represent your company, so you want them to be good. Blog content needs to be well-written and easy to read. Images need to be clear and have the right tone and message. And you need to embed your call to action.

Viral Content Basics

Headline and Title. Be clear and descriptive with an emotional hook. Include an SEO keyword or two that is part of your larger SEO strategy. Consider how it will appear and come across on various social media platforms. A fun example is "Skywalkers in Korea Cross Han Solo," which is really just a simple story about tightrope walkers crossing a river named Han as part of an annual festival. But that title makes you want to click and find out, right? Here's the story.

Text Readability. Viral content needs to be digestible by the masses, not only those interested in your niche and familiar with the jargon. You want the text to be readable. One way to check that is to have people outside of your business and industry read it and tell you what they do and do not understand. Another way is to gauge the grade level readability. You can check anything you can cut-and-paste or that has a URL here.

Highlight Importance. Back in 2008, Nielson found that, "On the average Web page, users have time to read at most 28% of the words during an average visit; 20% is more likely." With the advent of mobile and the rise of social media, that percentage is likely even lower these days. Use these text-formatting elements in the body of your post:

Sub-headings
Lists
Bullet points
Bold text
Underlined text

Start Strong. The first paragraph and/or the first 10 seconds is critical. You want to clearly indicate what your article or video is about right away. You also want to activate that emotional hook in the reader or viewer quickly. Attention fades fast. Make sure your key message and emotional hook are obvious from the outset.

Length. Long form blogging is more likely to be shared and go viral. This surprises most people; even bloggers. Why long content? Because it's obvious the author spent time and energy making it valuable. When you explain things in depth, people appreciate it, it's unexpected, and it's likely practical and useful — which people will instinctively know. Then those same people share it. For videos, short and long both work well. It's the middle that loses people. Short videos end under 5 minutes, so people know they can wedge it between other searches; long videos last around an hour, revealing an in-depth talk or lecture people can settle in for.

Images. People love pictures. If you go to Reddit, aka "The front page of the Internet," you'll see that more than half of the most popular content will be images. Smiling, happy people work well. Animals are great. Color goes a long way. Infographics and charts can spice up the driest numbers.

Share Buttons. Content that has a share button is shared seven times as much as content without them. You want to have share buttons that are easy to see and use — ideally at the top of the post or right next to your video. If you can embed share buttons in the content, that's even better.

Consistency and Authority. People act on trust and familiarity. It helps content get humming and on its viral way, especially during the first wave. Robert Caldini, Regents' Professor Emeritus of Psychology and Marketing at Arizona State University, says, "People prefer to say yes to those things that show strong consistency in their actions." You can use this to your advantage by having someone prominent or well-connected at your company author the post or be in the video and by making sure it's consistent with your other branding."

How to Create and Tell a Compelling Story

Being Personal

You might not care what the general perception of your brand is as long as people are buying from you, but most consumers tend to buy from the companies they like and trust. Thus, it's important to try and develop a personal relationship with your customers and get them to invest in your brand on an emotional level.

Try to always speak to the individual, not the crowd — mass marketing is no longer a successful practice in 2014. People want to be communicated with on a one-to-one basis, not feel like they are part of a group. When you watch something, listen to something, or read something, you're not digesting it as *we* or *you*, are digesting it as "*I.*" It's an old radio trick, but when someone wants to promote an event, they don't say, "we want to see you all at the event on Saturday," they say, "I want to meet you on Saturday and to have a cup of coffee with you and chat with you." Make it about "you" the person and "them" the person.

Having worked out your message, image, and overall persona, make sure to be as personable and relatable as possible. If your company is perceived as open and sharing, you're more likely to build a trustworthy relationship with your customers that's invaluable to your business. Sharing some of your story will help people feel like they know, relate to, and trust YOU.

Becoming a Contributor

Some people will tell you that the first step to PR is having your own blog; others tell you to think again. Having your own site and links to other sites is great, but you may not want to have your own blog. Keeping up a blog can be a great deal of work, and if you don't blog regularly, people will forget about it, and it will become a wasted resource. It may also take a long time to build a large audience.

Thus, your time is much better spent trying to get your brand featured in larger, more established publications. Whether you reach out to journalists or you get the opportunity to write your own articles, you will be able to reach a bigger audience much faster through outside publications. Furthermore, having your company featured in an established publication will add to your credibility, spread the word about your brand, and help you develop a stronger marketplace reputation.

Focus On Great Branding

First impressions count and your overall branding will be the first impression that people get of your startup. Consumers may see it at an event or online, but people do tend to judge a book by its cover. Make sure your logo is clear and easily recognizable. Spend some time and money on it, hire a designer, and make sure the end product is the exact visual representation of your brand and vision.

Other important aspects of branding are your tag line or slogan and your color scheme. Both of these things should tie into your logo and overall brand image and serve as supplemental elements that strengthen your brand identity. If your branding is poor, people will be quick to pass you off, but if your branding is on point, the sky's the limit — just look at what the "swoosh" did for Nike.

How to Handle Interviews

PR often requires meeting journalists and doing interviews. Before you do an interview, you should always research the person that is interviewing you, as well as what they write about. Google them and read their work. If the publication exposes a lot of negative aspects of other businesses or tends to be too harsh a critic, you might want to avoid the interview, especially in your early days. Most publishers and reporters, however, are not out to get you.

Ask in advance what the angle of the story is and what they are hoping to achieve from it. Make a list of what you do not want to talk about and make it a point to tell the reporter. On the other hand, you should also make a list of things you do want to talk about. If you can help the reporter get what they want for their readers and effectively deliver the points you want to make, then you both win. If they like you, you can be a resource they come back to later for more information or content.

10 Ways to Build Your Fan Base

"Social media has nothing to do with what you say about yourself and everything to do with what other people say about you" – Cynthia Johnson, Director of Social Media Marketing at RankLab and Editorial Director at Social Media Club

Since the advent of Facebook, Twitter, YouTube, and the rest of the social media platforms, it has never been easier to create and share digital content, communicate with fans directly, and amass a large online following. However, while these social media platforms have enabled brands to reach larger audiences than ever before, that doesn't mean that generating a fan base is a simple task. In fact, building a large and engaged online fan base takes time, effort, and quite a bit of strategy. However, armed with the right tools and knowledge, you too can build your own fan base. Here are 10 great ways to build a large and engaged online fan base.

1. **Create Unique Content.** As technology continues to advance, it becomes easier to create content and share it with the world. Although this may make your job easier to some extent, it's also making it easier for thousands of other people to create content as well. Thus, you have to find a way to offer users content they simply can't get anywhere else; you need to cut through all of the noise and be one of a kind. Know your niche, develop a strategy, and create content with your own unique perspective or focus. If you create content unlike anyone else, it will only be a matter of time before people start coming to your page and clicking the "like" or "follow" button.

2. **Interact With Your Fans.** Numerous companies seem to take this ability for granted, but social media has allowed brands to directly communicate with their followers like never before. Use this to your advantage and connect with people. The more interaction outsiders see, they more willing they will be to interact and engage with you and your page, and ultimately become a follower.

3. **Collaborate.** One of the easiest ways to build credibility within your space, network with likeminded people, and reach a larger audience overall is to collaborate with others. Collaborating is an easy way to get your name in front of people who otherwise might not have heard about you, while also establishing a positive relationship with a brand or person in your space.

4. **Offer Incentives.** Many businesses utilize things like "fan gates" to offer incentives to join. Components like fan gating allow you to offer exclusive content to your existing fans while enticing new fans to like your pages and view or receive your exclusive content. This is a great way to build your fan base and keep them engaged by sharing content strictly with them.

5. **Stay Current.** Staying up-to-date with current online trends is a quick and easy way to entertain and engage with an audience. Most have witnessed the power of a clever meme or a viral video and can attract new fans quickly and easily by taking advantage of current pop culture phenomena. Use tools such as Google Trends to stay current, and share content that relates to those trends.

6. **Use Contests.** Contests, sweepstakes, or promotions are often useful ways to grab the attention of would-be fans. Offer great deals or special content in a competitive and engaging format, and encourage people to interact with your brand that way. Again, this is a relatively simple way to grab the attention of new fans and offer them an exciting way to connect with your brand. A particularly good way to gain fans is by creating social media contests that require users to share your post with their own friends and followers to take part in the contest. Not only does this provide a great avenue for interacting with your fans, but it will also help spread your brand and content to a wider-reaching audience.

7. **Take Advantage of Free Tools.** There are a plethora of free tools on the Internet that put your brand in front of people and get them to interact with you, and you should be using them to your advantage. One great example is the Facebook Questions feature, which allows you to ask your fans anything you want and learn more about them, connect with them, and drive engagement. Keep current events in mind and ask your fans questions that they care about or are likely to have an opinion on regardless of your business. A great example that would drive traffic and encourage interaction would be a thought-provoking question about the government shutdown.

8. **Use Facebook Ads.** With the inclusion of Facebook's new advertising tools, creating targeted and effective ad campaigns is both easy and cheap. With Facebook ads, you can target your demographic very specifically and spend as little as $1 a day. Plus, if your Facebook ad is promoting your unique, exclusive content or some great deals from your business, it will likely drive more traffic and engagement.

9. **Use Twitter and Pinterest Effectively.** This book has focused quite a bit on Facebook so far, and rightfully so — it's a massive network with millions of highly engaged and targetable users. However, Facebook isn't the only social network on the block, and platforms such as Twitter and Pinterest provide their own benefits for growing your fan base. But to be successful on these two networks, you must understand how they

work and what drives engagement. On Twitter, "retweets" are often a great way to interact with other users, collaborate with likeminded users, and get your brand in front of more people. The more you retweet other people, the more likely they are to follow you and retweet your posts as well. With Pinterest, you must know that a vast majority of pinned content is re-pinned. So, if you are able to create visually impressive and witty Pinterest posts, it's likely that you will get re-pinned and reach a larger audience.

10. **Use Your Fans as Marketers.** One of the most effective ways to use social media to build your fan base is to let your followers spread your brand and do the heavy lifting for you. As long as you employ the tips listed above — create unique content, use contests, share memes, ask questions — you will develop a highly engaged fan base that will be enticed by your posts and more likely to share them with their own friends. Remember that if you create shareable, exciting, and fresh content, people will want to share it, and that's how you can grow your network.

If you're starting a fan page or a business from scratch, there's no doubt that reaching new fans and building a sizable audience is a daunting task. However, with social media and various tools online, it's never been easier to reach the masses. Use some of the tips here and chances are you'll have a decent sized fan base in a relatively short period of time.

Chapter Six:

Developing Your PR Strategies

Building a connection with PR specialists and industry influencers is not an easy feat. Keep in mind, there's a big difference between "following" and "stalking." For your PR campaign to work effectively, you need to develop a strategy.

It's a no-brainer that you need an effective plan for your business to succeed. The same thing goes for public relations. An effective PR campaign requires an equally effective campaign strategy to work.

So how can you develop a PR campaign that works?

Define Your PR Campaign's Objectives

When creating a PR strategy for your business, the first thing you need to do is define your objectives. Your goal will serve as your guide towards what you want to achieve for your brand, as well as the resources you are going to need and when you are going to need them.

In addition, having a goal unifies your team. When your team knows your business goals, it allows them to bear in mind what is expected of them. It also helps improve communication between participants. Simply put, having a goal allows you to create measurable results.

To create an effective PR campaign objective, it should answer the question "What do I want to get out of this?" The answer could be any of the following:

Increase Brand Awareness

PR gives your business the exposure it deserves. This is an important step, especially if you want to raise awareness for a startup that has not yet established a strong recognition in the market.

Drive More Traffic or Sales

When more and more people get to know your brand through PR, there is a possibility that these people will check out your business to see what you can offer. If your content convinces them that you have the solution to their problems, your audience is more likely to hit the "buy" button.

Boost Your Website's SEO

PR can boost your website's search engine optimization campaign. With the exposure your business gets through PR, links from external sites (also known as inbound links) will start to pour in. These inbound links serve as a vote of confidence on your website, especially in terms of how relevant your content is with the subject matter (in this case, the term or keyword an Internet user types in the search box).

Promote a New Product or Service

PR is all about creating brand awareness, but it's not purely about promoting a startup. It can also help you promote a new product or service. This is possible because PR allows you to build trust among your audience and establish your business' credibility.

Demonstrate Thought Leadership

Although PR is known more for promoting a business, it can also serve as a way for you to demonstrate thought leadership. Showcasing your expertise by sending out useful information to your audience regularly allows you to be memorable with your target customers.

Improve Personal Branding

Aside from promoting your brand, PR has the capacity to change people's attitude towards your business — especially if your company is struggling with negative perception. PR allows your audience to understand your message and resolve issues.

According to Kim Harrison of Cutting Edge PR, "goals are the means to express the end points towards which effort is directed." Imagine your PR campaign's objectives as the end of the road — your destination. Without it, you will never know what road to take to get there.

Outline Your Plan

Once you've identified your PR campaign's objectives, the next thing you need to do is outline your plan. As previously mentioned, your objective is your destination. Your plan, on the other hand, is the road you need to take to get to your destination.

Outlining your plan is an important element of an effective PR strategy. This allows you to make sure that everyone in your team is in agreement with your objectives, as well as the tactics and resources you will need to achieve your goals.

Elements of a PR Plan

The reason you actually get down to business is to create an effective communication plan that will help get your message to the right audience. To meet your campaign's objective, you have to make sure your plan contains the following elements:

Target Audience or Market

If you determine your business' niche, chances are you have already identified your target audience. However, being "everything to everyone" is a no-no in public relations — even if you already have an *idea* of who your audience will be.

HubSpot CMO Mike Volpe advises that you "get persona-fied." Instead of saying that your business' target audience are condo-dwelling families in San Francisco (because there could be hundreds of them), create a clear buying persona and build your promotional strategy around them.

A persona includes demographics, age, buying habits, and other relevant information that will guide your PR campaign. You can even give it a name if you want. Think of your buying persona as a Facebook account.

Let's say your target customer is John. He is 35-years old and lives with his wife and three-year-old son in a condo unit somewhere in San Francisco, California. What does he do for a living? What are his hobbies? What are the books, magazines, or blogs he usually reads?

This information will help you point out John's predicament or what makes his life quite difficult, as well as how you can get his attention towards your content.

Once you have identified your business' buying persona, it will be easier for you to build appropriate promotional strategies around your target audience – just because you already know how your business can address their needs.

Influencers

Industry influencers are basically people with a significant following. You need to connect with them because they can help bring your message to more people. But identifying important voices in your niche is not solely based on whether they have hundreds or thousands of followers on Twitter.

Ask yourself the following questions when seeking that known personality with whom you want to be associated:

1. Do they share the same values and support similar advocacies as yours?

2. Do they share relevant information regarding your business niche?

3. Are their followers also your target audience?

The good thing is that there are available tools which allow you to track influencers who can help spread the message for you.

Once you have identified the industry influencer with whom you wish to be associated, you can start connecting with them through online platforms or networking events. You can follow the same rules of engagement with PR professionals that were previously mentioned in this book.

The bottom line: You should identify the personalities who can help you connect with your target audience and bring in the right traffic, and reach out to them without being bothersome.

Key Message

Your key message, or your marketing pitch, is the most important part of your campaign because this will help people create an impression about your business. There are two things you need to keep in mind when creating your business' key message:

1. It should reflect your campaign's objective.

2. It should be tailored for your target audience.

To make it simple, the message you want to bring to the industry should answer the question "What do you want your audience and the media to remember about you?"

If you want to be remembered as a businessperson who sells eco-friendly air conditioning units, your key message should revolve around your company's most important aspects. This could include the importance of environment-friendly devices, how your products and services contribute to this advocacy, how it can help your consumers, and if these services are also available for small-to-medium businesses or enterprises.

Remember to make your key message significant to avoid confusion regarding your company's identity. Otherwise, it will decrease your business' value proposition.

Platform

As mentioned earlier in this book, public relations is a form of marketing that allows a company to receive editorial coverage. However, advances in technology have changed the way businesses do PR — including the platforms you can use to establish your presence in the industry.

1. **Social Media.** An incredibly useful tool for spreading your business message across the Internet, social media enables you to interact with your audience in a personal way.

2. **Blogs and Websites.** As with social media, blogs and websites can help globalize your business through the Internet — only they provide a wider avenue. While social networking sites allows you to interact with your target audience, blogs and websites allow you to showcase your expertise online.

3. **Newsletters.** If social media makes communication human and websites let you showcase your expertise, then newsletters make the experience more intimate. By sending newsletters to your existing audience, you send exclusive information straight to them. And who does not love exclusive offers?

4. **Public Events.** Another way to gain exposure for your business is by attending public events. You do not have to strike a speaking deal immediately, though. What's

important is that you meet like-minded people and have face-to-face interaction with them.

5. **Traditional Media.** Communicating through traditional media such as newspaper, magazine, TV, and radio may be old school, but this tactic still proves effective. People consider information through these channels as being trustworthy and more meaningful than paid ads.

Good public relations is a complex process, especially if you are doing it for your startup. By having an effective campaign strategy and knowing which platforms to use, you can reach your target audience and get your business known to them.

Key Metrics

Identifying which metrics to measure is important simply because it lets you know whether your strategies are effective or not. Without it, you will never know if you need to move forward with your campaign or sit back and see if changes are needed to make a workaround.

Your PR campaign's key metrics can include the following:

1. Interaction

The great thing about public relations is that it also allows you to listen to what your target audience has to say about you, your brand, and the products and services you offer.

Track which among your messages resonate best with them and which fall on deaf ears. You should also consider how they react to your marketing pitch. Did your message compel them to share information with their friends? How many of your contacts replied and asked for more information? Did you receive hate messages afterwards?

Having an idea of how your audience reacts to your messages allows you to refine your pitches over time.

2. Reach and Coverage

It's okay to keep in mind that news will spread on its own, especially if it's something newsworthy like a viral video on YouTube. However, it's important to know where the news is heading.

Consider how many people are talking about your news, who they are, and how influential they are. This helps you determine the type of audience that really consumes whatever content you send out, as well as the personalities who can help you reach those people.

You should also check out the medium where your news is spreading and how popular that medium is to your audience. Just because Facebook and Twitter are the most popular social networks on the Web does not mean they can help spread the message for you.

If your business targets other businesses or professionals, LinkedIn might be a useful social network for you. The same goes for Pinterest and Instagram if your target audience prefers visual content over plain text.

3. Traffic and Sales

Measuring who consumes your content, where they get it, and how they interact with it is merely the beginning. You should also measure whether the exposure you garner brings in leads or people who could be interested in the products or services you offer.

In relation to that, you have to track how many of your leads clicked the "buy" button. This is not only about how much revenue your PR campaign brings in, but also determining who really needs the products and services your offer and why they need it.

In summary, the metrics you will need to measure depend on your PR campaign objectives. These metrics will help you determine whether your strategies are meeting your expectations or not. They let you know which among your strategies keep you on track to reach your business' goals.

Having a proper plan can determine whether your PR campaign is going to succeed or not. Without it, you will never know the appropriate steps to take to achieve your business goals, the impression you want your business to create, the message you want your brand to communicate, or the metrics of success you want to measure.

Execute Your Plan

Now you have your goals and your plans on how you can achieve success. The next thing you need to do is take action.

Before you reach out to influencers, appreciate their point of view recommends Actionable Marketing Guide's Heidi Cohen. This translates to looking them up via Google, their website, blog, and social media. *Understand that your desire for their support may not be aligned with their own objectives.*

Take the time to build a relationship with each influencer separately. In Cohen's view, you need to pay-it-forward by commenting on their blog posts and articles as well as sharing their social communications to attract their attention. Otherwise you risk that you email will automatically get deleted.

When reaching out to influencers, think about your request from their perspective. Does you inquiry answer "What's in it for them?" If not, answer that question before sending your request.

There are four things you can do to execute your plan:

1. Develop and Share Your Brand's Story

As mentioned earlier, tell your influencers and target market what you or your products can do for them. Perfect your pitch element.

Instead of showing how your product works, share the story behind it. Why did you create it in the first place?

Articulate on your business goals and focus on how they will benefit your market.

2. Connect With Your Network

Connecting with your network allows you to improve your reputation in your niche. But for you to enhance your brand and meet your goals, you will need your network's help.

Don't hesitate to ask them to share information about your business, products, and services. Better yet, ask your network how you can help them. That way, you can alleviate their pain points and showcase your expertise at the same time.

3. Do a Follow Up

PR works best when there's a follow up marketing strategy that can boost and extend your campaign's shelf life. To do this, use your website to promote any press release or article mentions you receive.

You can also take advantage of the power of social media. Has someone on Twitter said something good about you? Give that user a retweet!

Other than that, you can share your PR pieces on your social networks, which allow your followers to read and share with people connected to them. In the end, it doesn't only make your campaign live longer, it also leverages your brand.

4. Keep in Touch With Influencers

While one way to generate PR for your startup is through industry influencers, it's not advisable to connect with them only when you need their popularity. Remember, PR is all about building relationships.

If they ask a question or seek help, don't hesitate to raise a hand and volunteer. If they'll be at an industry or networking event, take the time to attend and meet up with them. Commend their keynote and share your thoughts. Read and comment intelligibly on their posts if they also write for relevant websites.

The key here is to always be within their radar. That way, it will be easier for you to reach out to them the next time you need coverage.

More important than getting your business known to PR specialists and influencers, it's best to get your brand known for what it can do for their audience. This will help you gain their support and, in the end, compel them to give the spotlight your company deserves.

Chapter Seven:
Building a Network With PR
Professionals

People in the public relations industry receive hundreds if not thousands of marketing pitches every week. Therefore, it's vital to connect with the appropriate PR pros.

There are three simple ways your brand can stand out from the sea of marketing pitches:

Identify Your Connection

The first thing you need to do when building a network with PR specialists is to identify with whom you wish to be associated.

With the help of social networking sites like Facebook, Twitter, and LinkedIn, look for journalists who share news and stories relevant to your niche. Check out whether they support the same advocacies you support. Follow them on every social media channel they are in, and interact with them by exchanging comments and information regarding your shared industry.

If they ask a question that you can answer, for instance, do not hesitate to share what you know. It would be even better if you have the resources they are seeking. At this point, you are not only building a connection but also becoming a thought leader in your industry.

Make Face-to-Face Interaction

Talking to professionals and specialists online is not enough, especially if you have the opportunity to meet face-to-face. Nothing can beat a personal interaction.

Is your favorite journalist going to speak at an event?

Will such an event allow you to meet and connect with like-minded people?

If your answer to both questions is "yes," then there is no reason for you to stay at home and not grab the opportunity to build a network of like-minded people.

Other than connecting with PR professionals and known thought leaders in your industry, face-to-face interaction allows you to crowdsource what your industry might need and how your business can address it.

Explain What You Can Do... For Them

This is where you can use that pitch you have been practicing for days and weeks. However, a simple answer such as "I sell AC units with plasma filters" can be boring.

"What do you do?" is already a simple question. Make it colorful by giving an interesting answer. Instead of telling people what you do, explain what you can do for them.

Tell them, "I help clean the air by providing AC units with plasma filters." Then you can explain the benefits of plasma filters and how they clean the air. You can even follow it up by expressing the benefits of clean air to people and the environment.

The key here is to make your pitch as creative as possible, so it can prompt other people to ask follow up questions — making the discussion entertaining and educational at the same time. It's all about finding the opportunity to share what you know.

As mentioned again and again in this book, public relations is about building relationships with specialists and industry influencers. But more than that, PR finds and connects you with people who share the same beliefs. For you to build that connection with PR professionals, you need to identify first with whom you wish to be associated.

With the help of social media, look for journalists or specialists who are relevant to your brand or niche. Follow them on social networking sites and interact with them by exchanging comments and information regarding your shared industry.

However, be careful not to sound salesy. Instead of saying that you have such and such product or you offer this and that kind of services, why not offer your help? Explain how you can make their lives easier rather than merely stating what you can do. It's like building a trade of sorts, which will eventually allow you to earn their support and trust. It's more likely for journalists and PR professionals to promote your brand, your products, or services that way rather than cold pitching it to them.

The Appropriate Way to Contact the Press

Once you have appropriate, timely, and well-developed content ready for distribution and publication, the focus shifts from internal to external. It's no longer about developing an idea, delivering a pitch to top-level management, producing content, and editing work; it now comes down to contacting people who can connect you with your target audience.

Understanding the Press

There are many common misconceptions about the press. They are often presented as biased, cold-hearted, and ruthless, but those are unfair attributions. Rather, most companies simply don't know how to properly approach the press in a manner that is respectful and effective.

By putting yourself in the shoes of the press, you can better understand the way they operate, what their motives are, and how to tailor your approach accordingly. Here are some things you must know about the press:

- **You Aren't Everything.** While some sources are looking for work on a continual basis, others are busy and occupied. You have to understand that editors, writers, and publishers get many emails, phone calls, and offers. Just because you've spent the last few hours, days, or weeks developing a release doesn't mean everyone feels as strongly about your idea as you do. Once you leave the friendly confines of your own business, it can be a tough fight to gain visibility.

- **First Impressions Are Everything.** Most people with a business background understand this concept, but first impressions are everything. If your idea doesn't interest the person on the receiving end within seconds or minutes, you will probably end up at the bottom of a long stack of other boring content. An engaging opening line is vital.

- **Specialization.** Just as you specialize in the work you do, most members of the press do as well. Your content may not work with every outlet, so research who you are contacting. For example, if your company sells musical instruments and you want to distribute a press release announcing the opening of a new location, your contacts are limited. You could contact local business publications, music websites, and other similar sources, but contacting financial publications, entertainment magazines, and literary agencies is a waste of time. You cannot take a shotgun approach with the press.

- **Newsworthy.** The press wants to distribute newsworthy material as much as you want to produce newsworthy content. Unless you are going after a distribution source that largely pushes personal interest content, you aren't going to have much success unless your material is newsworthy and engaging to readers.

- **Understand the Process.** While there are a number of ways to contact the press, email is one of the primary methods. With that being said, it would benefit you to understand what happens when you email an idea to a member of the press. The process usually looks like this: (1) The email goes directly to the recipient's inbox. (2) Either the recipient himself or an assistant quickly scans the subject line and sender information. (3) The email is either opened, saved for later, or immediately discarded. (4) If opened, the recipient reads the first couple of sentences, scans through the rest of it, and quickly makes an assessment. (5) If the assistant finds it valuable, the email is forwarded to the appropriate source. If the recipient himself finds it valuable, other attachments, screenshots, videos, and links are analyzed. (6) If the opportunity is deemed valuable, follow up contact is made.

How to Contact the Press

While the above example makes the process sound simple and streamlined, contacting the press involves a number of steps and additional effort. There is no cookie cutter method for appropriately contacting the press, but there are some factors that increase the likelihood of success.

Step 1: Preparation

Doing your homework will take you a long way. As mentioned, most distribution sources are highly specialized and only publish certain types of content. If you contact a source that does not distribute the type of content you have, it appears rude and unprofessional. You can avoid wasting the time of others by doing some simple research. Many industries release press guides that list appropriate media sources, but if not, keep track on your own.

The best way to keep track of media sources that may be valuable is by keeping an updated spreadsheet with notes, contact information, and other pertinent details. In addition to choosing sources that mesh with your content, you also need to review the form of content they publish. Do they strictly push press releases? Or, are they heavily focused on news articles and interviews?

Step 2: Structure

Once you have developed an accurate and precise list of potential contacts, it's important to structure your plan of attack. If you are going the email route, formatting is extremely important. As the previous example mentioned, you only have a few seconds or words to prove value.

The idea is to immediately engage the recipient in a friendly tone. The beginning of your email should be concise, yet complete. Then, if the recipient wants to learn more, they can continue reading. If possible, include valuable graphics, information, links, videos, etc., but don't overdo it! Too many attachments and elements can be overwhelming and send off too strong of a signal.

Step 3: Content

Going hand-in-hand with the structure is the content. As mentioned, it needs to be engaging and informative. Very rarely will a member of the press ask for clarification after the first contact. Your content should be clear and easily understood.

It's also important to add some personalization to your content. While you may be sending similar inquiries to multiple sources, each recipient should feel like you spent time hand-crafting content especially for them. It's not enough to include their name; subtly embed references that show you are familiar with who they are, what they do, or what they stand for.

Lastly, the recipient should understand your personal goals. They should know what timeframe you are looking to target, who your intended audience is, what your expectations are, and why you chose to contact them.

Step 4: Delivery
Once you've crafted a well-developed, personalized, highly engaging contact strategy, it's time to deliver. This is generally the easy part, as preparation has already been completed. If your goal is to be timely with the information or content, your delivery should be as well. Try to reach all contacts within the same timeframe to ensure nobody is behind.

Other Tips For Appropriately Contacting the Press

Successfully contacting the press is not about sending hundreds of pitches and bombarding journalists with useless information. It's about sending out highly targeted, well-developed pitches to the **right** contacts. More tips for making the most of your time include:

- **Give and Take.** Prove you are willing to give and take. When contacting the press, your success is largely dependent upon your ability to suggest mutually beneficial results.

- **Be Specific.** Instead of telling someone your past content has improved readership for publications, say "XYZ article improved readership by ABC percent for 123 News Publication."

- **Be Professional.** Nothing is a bigger turnoff than receiving a pitch full of grammatical errors, inconsistencies, and unfinished thoughts. Be careful and only send out professional and accurate content.

What Not to Do
Just as there is a long list of what you should do, there are also a number of things you will want to avoid when contacting the press.

- **Don't Be Annoying.** It's your job to be persistent, not annoying. If you are constantly beating down the doors, you probably aren't going to be let in. Instead, follow the "drip" methodology, which says continual, steady contact is the best.

- **Don't Use Overkill.** While spreadsheets, graphics, and videos can be interesting and effective, don't take it too far. You'll end up overwhelming the recipient and missing the mark.

- **Don't be Corporate.** The biggest piece of advice to remember is to avoid being corporate. Your target is a person and deserves to be treated like a person. There is a difference between being corporate and professional. Being professional means you are respectful, careful, and courteous. Being corporate means you act like a robot or computer and show no emotion.

There are right and wrong ways to contact the press. While every member of the press operates differently, consistent success is possible by heeding this advice and approaching with careful preparation.

Building Relationships and Not Merely Contacts

Clearly, public relations is less about the type of content and material you produce and more about how well you connect with people. It's a question that permeates every area of business: How do you develop long-lasting, healthy, beneficial relationships?

The Heart of Public Relations

Back in 1982, the Public Relations Society of America formally adopted an official definition of public relations. It read, "Public relations helps an organization and its publics adapt mutually to each other." While the definition was not technically wrong or misguided, it did a disservice to what public relations really stands for.

Because of that, the Public Relations Society of America decided to modernize the definition in 2012. To allow all voices to be heard, they conducted a crowdsourcing campaign and took a public vote on the new definition. It now reads, "Public relations is a strategic communication process that builds mutually beneficial relationships between organizations and their publics."

At the heart of that definition is the phrase "builds mutually beneficial relationships." That's what PR is all about. It's not only a way of using contacts to bark at a captive audience. Rather, it involves developing healthy relationships with members of the media, as well as the target audience.

If PR was strictly focused on "strategic communication," things would look different. Your goal would be to develop a long list of contacts and connections that could strategically benefit and profit your company. However, successful PR requires a much more intricate and personalized approach.

The Difference Between Contacts and Relationships

It's uncanny how often the business world mirrors our personal lives. Once again, we see reflections and metaphors when analyzing relationships. In your personal life, you likely have loved ones, friends, and acquaintances. Each has their benefits and limitations, but they are all quite different from each other.

An acquaintance is someone you merely know of or come into contact with occasionally. These are the people you say hello to, but the conversation usually doesn't go any further. You may even question whether or not to acknowledge them when you see each other in passing. In these situations, it's unclear of where the relationship stands, how you should appropriately interact, or whether there is any future ahead. Regardless of how these emotions and understandings stack up, it's generally understood that you aren't good friends. You probably won't go out of your way to do something for them, and vice versa.

Your friends are those people with whom you have history, interact with frequently, and genuinely enjoy being around. Friendships also have a variety of levels, but generally speaking, you are comfortable around these people and are able to carry on interesting, meaningful, or natural conversations. As opposed to the awkwardness of acquaintances, you have a rather clear understanding of how you should interact with a friend. You may go out of your way to help them out with something, and they would probably do the same.

Loved ones would be classified as extremely close friends and family members. These are the people included in your inner circle. They have some sort of stake in your life and have a commitment to see you achieve health and success. Typically, you don't have much of a choice in who your loved ones are. These are usually people you gain access to through blood relation, or those you've spent much of your life around.

How does all this relate back to PR? It's simple. Business relationships are similar to personal relationships. You likely have individuals in all three categories and interact with each group differently.

In the business landscape, there are acquaintances, contacts, and relationships. Acquaintances are those companies or individuals you have crossed paths with in the past. They may indirectly work with you on certain projects or they may merely be a member of the same industry or community. Business acquaintances sometimes turn into contacts, but usually stay put.

Contacts are those individuals or companies that you work with on a semi-regular to regular basis. You have their contact information, know how to get in touch with them, and can reach out with little effort. While you may work with or receive occasional assistance from contacts, the relationship is limited in what can be done. Your contacts probably won't offer much extra effort when you need it.

Relationships — as they do in personal life — take work in the business world. These are the individuals or companies you frequently work with, know on a personal level, and trust to some degree. Business relationships are where you turn when you need help, assistance, or guidance.

As you can see, there is stark difference between contacts and relationships. In public relations, you cannot thrive without having relationships with members of the press and media. If all you have are contacts, you will be severely limited in what you will accomplish. Take the time to develop business relationships, not piles of dusty business cards.

8 Tips for Building Relationships

Don't underestimate the difficulty of building quality relationships, but do invest time and resources in doing so. Here are eight tips for building healthy and effective business relationships with members of the press.

- **Be Personal.** In a world of social media communication, email, and texting, it's often difficult to make any real connection with someone. Instead of always relying on LinkedIn or email to build business relationships, how about picking up the phone and making a call? What about setting up a lunch meeting? Remember, you are trying to move from contact to relationship. You can't treat the latter like the former and expect it to bear fruit.

- **Be Regular.** While business relationships are different than personal relationships on many levels, there are a number of similarities. As you must put in time to grow personal relationships, you must also put in regular effort to build business relationships. This looks a little different in the business world — and you can't realistically spend hours each day networking with one individual — but trying to schedule regular interactions is good. Maybe it's a lunch meeting once a month. Whatever it is, there needs to be some consistency.

- **Clarity is Key.** The major difference between business relationships and personal relationships is that something more than pure enjoyment is at stake. You aren't simply interacting with business relationships for fun; rather, you both want something in return. In public relations, you are looking for an outlet to distribute content. Members of the press are looking for high quality content to fill space and attract advertising. It's okay to be clear on what the goals are.

- **Do Interviews.** If you are looking for an extremely tangible way to build rapport with a member of the press, consider allowing an interview. Most business journalists are constantly on the prowl for interviews and case studies. If you are willing to provide information like this on an occasional basis, they will likely give you a little exposure in return.

- **Show More than Respect.** While respect is an important part of business relationships, it certainly isn't everything. Members of the press want respect from the subjects they cover, but also want some personality. If all you ever offer are cold, hard facts, it's going to be difficult to develop rapport. Ease the stiffness, and let them in on the details.

- **Ask for Suggestions.** While you may always feel like you have killer pitches and ideas, it's important to understand that you don't work **in** the press — only **with** it. As a way to show your appreciation for those in the press, ask them for suggestions occasionally. They possess a deep knowledge of their audience and can point you in the right direction. In addition to being able to better target pitches, you will show respect for their opinion.

- **Get the Name Down.** Often, the only difference between acquaintances and relationships is knowing the other individual's name. When you are on a first name basis, your pitches are noticed, inquires get responses, and contacts become relationships.

- **Don't Get Pushy.** Understand nuance and recognize when you're pushing too hard. Relationships aren't built overnight; take the slow and steady approach. Be personal and consistent, but don't overstep your boundaries.

At the heart of public relations is the idea of building relationships, not merely contacts. When you interact with the press, be sure to approach it from a personal, mutually beneficial angle. Your ability to build quality relationships will be one of the most important factors of your PR success.

How to Leverage Relationships

Once you have established relationships with members of the press, it's important to learn how to leverage them for optimal success. A relationship in and of itself will not benefit you much. You must learn to find value and extract it. From a public relations standpoint, you can effectively leverage relationships to drive traffic, improve conversions, and increase search engine rankings.

Driving Traffic

An effective working relationship with the press will allow you to consistently drive traffic to your website. While you still need high quality content, marketing, and advertising, your relational foundation will play a major role in driving traffic. Here are some specific ways to leverage relationships to drive traffic:

- **Distribute Press Releases.** Many people incorrectly believe public relations only involves producing press releases. Seen as official, factual, and professional, press releases certainly have their place and can rise above other forms of content on the basis of authority — if distributed properly. If you locate a visible outlet for press releases, you should see a bump in site traffic. Readers will be naturally curious about your company after reading a well-written release and may click through to find out more.

- **Reciprocate.** As previously mentioned, there should be some give and take when it comes to working relationships with the press. If you really want to leverage relationships, offer free content in return for exposure. You can even stipulate that content must contain X backlinks and Y brand mentions. Be sure to always reciprocate favors.

- **Take Advice.** Nobody understands what readers like, want, and need like the media. If you are getting advice from trusted connections, take it. They almost always point you in the right direction and help you avoid straying too far.

- **Develop Viral Content.** The beauty of the Internet — from a PR, advertising, or marketing point of view — is that content can go viral in a matter of minutes or hours. Leverage your relationships to develop high quality content and distribute it through the right channels. Often times, the most basic channels work best; such as Facebook, Twitter, and other popular sharing sites.

- **Build a Network.** If you have done a good job developing a positive rapport with one individual, you may be able to capitalize on their other connections. Building a network of press relationships allows you to steadily build backlinks and increase site traffic.

To Increase Conversions

Regardless of your conversion objectives, business relationships will be your best aid in reaching these goals. To best leverage relationships and increase conversions, consider the following:

- **Openly Communicate.** When offering interviews or pitches to your contacts in the press, use relationships to your advantage. Done correctly, you should be able to bargain for particular stipulations. This can help increase conversions. For example, if you are looking to sell more of product XYZ, ask if they can subtly plug product XYZ in the next piece published.

- **Ride the Coattail.** While you can't ride someone's coattail consistently, it does work from time to time. If you have a relationship with a respected member of the media, use it to your advantage. Ask them if they can mention something that would increase conversions on your end. Loyal followers trust their favorite members of the press.

- **Effective Headlines.** For those that write for a living, crafting effective, catchy headlines comes naturally. While you may have a killer pitch, is your headline on par? If not, you may be able to leverage your relationships to obtain well-crafted headlines that increase conversions.

To Increase Search Engine Rankings

One of the most important factors in a company's success on the Internet is its ability to rise in search engine rankings and land on the first page of Google for particular keywords. Here are a few tips on how you can leverage relationships to increase search engine rankings:

- **Develop Backlinks.** In addition to the exposure press releases, articles, blogs, and other forms of Internet content give a company or brand, there is value in the links contained within the actual text. Google — and other search engines — use backlinks as one of the primary ways to determine a web page's authority. If you can leverage your relationships to include credible backlinks, you will almost certainly see an increase in rankings.

- **Diversification.** The more relationships you have, the more success you will experience, as your rankings largely depend on the diversity of your backlinks. Each connection will develop different types of links, such as links on educational pages, links in blogs, links in press releases, etc.

- **Authority.** You could personally publish a piece of content and it wouldn't do nearly as well as if a reputable member of the press published it. Authority matters to Google, and you can benefit greatly by linking up with authoritative figures. This is a sure-fire way to increase search engine rankings.

Chapter Eight:
Creating an Effective Follow-Up Strategy

Perhaps one of the reasons startups fail is because they are content with the first sale. What they fail to realize, though, is that this is only the beginning.

When it comes to starting up a business and selling products or services, most business owners focus only on the product, how to promote it, and the revenue it brings in. However, the real money is in the follow-up.

As mentioned earlier in this book, public relations works best when there is a follow up marketing strategy that can boost and extend your campaign's shelf life.

Provide Customer Support

No matter how much time you spend perfecting your products or services, there will always be a customer with a question; not because there is a problem (although it does happen), but because there will always be unanswered queries.

You can take advantage of your customers' curiosity by providing customer support. Give them ways they can contact you if the need arises. In relation to this, always have a team trained and ready to solve customer issues.

Another thing to do is give your customers a personal call or send a "just checking in" letter or e-mail that usually goes out a couple of days after the purchase. Check out whether your customers are satisfied with your products or services, and inquire if they are having an issue with it or not.

You not only determine if you hit the target with your products and services, but make yourself approachable to customers.

Talk About the Natural Next Step

Most startups offer an introductory price for their products and services. It's usually followed by an e-mail campaign to offer complementary products or services.

However, being blunt and saying "buy this" is a not advisable in public relations — even more so when you are conducting a follow-up campaign. Instead, talk about the natural next step in which your customers can engage to take full advantage of your products or services.

What is wonderful about this tactic is that you can build a network of loyal customers while establishing your company as a premier provider. Because of the complementary products and services you provide, your customers will no longer need to go elsewhere for support.

Always Ask For Suggestions

Another way to employ an effective follow up strategy is to let your customers say what is on their mind. You can provide your contact information for customers to use if they would like to suggest something.

Other than that, you can always take advantage of social media. With the help of third-party apps or online services, you can use your social network accounts to check out what your existing customers have to say about your product. Better yet, ask your network what else they would like to see from your business.

Bottom line: Always take the time to listen to your customers' sentiments and see how your business can address any suggestions.

Maximizing the Value of Media Coverage

Once your startup has developed its story and branding and generated some media coverage, it's important to leverage that press to accelerate the growth of your business. Here are some ways you can optimize your media coverage and take advantage of positive PR:

- **Make a Positive Comment and Encourage Fans to Do the Same.** When you receive media coverage, you should always promote it across your various channels. It's much more beneficial to your business and more interesting from a customer's perspective when you promote content that someone else has written about your company. And, in the case that someone comments on it, you should take that opportunity to engage with those comments and build a personal relationship with your fans!

- **Share it on Your Social Pages and in Relevant Groups.** Share it with your fans several times, as not everyone sees every Facebook page post. Do the same on Twitter. Consider making it a promoted post or Tweet. Use other networks like LinkedIn, Google+, or Pinterest, depending on the coverage. If you have fans that have their own followings, ask them to do the same.

- **Share it on Your Site.** Write a short introduction to the piece on your website and link to it. Why would you want to create content that your audience can't find? Regardless of where it's posted, always make sure your network and audience know about your content.

- **Include it in Your Email Newsletter**. As a startup, you probably have an email list of past users and potential customers. Share your media coverage with them in your next newsletter. Another successful approach is to add a link to your content in the footer of your email signature — let it be the last link people see, and they will hopefully be encouraged to follow it.

- **If You're Interviewed on Camera, Promote it With YouTube Ads.** YouTube is fast becoming an essential marketing channel, so if the content about your brand is already there, why not find a better way to spread it further? Linking to a YouTube channel or specific video is a good way to drive traffic and increase views, which often leads to users sharing your video content. Remember to message your YouTube subscribers about your video and ask them to comment, like, and share as well.

If you're able to do all of this and drive new traffic to a publication, you shouldn't be surprised if you get opportunities to receive more coverage. If you're looking for further press coverage, sharing previous success stories will only promote your credibility and help you land pieces on more publications across the web. Showing that you know how to work with publishers is one of the best ways to garner more opportunities with them.

Press Releases

What is a Press Release?

One of the most effective ways you can get the message out about your brand is through a press release. A press release is simply "a written or recorded communication directed at members of the news media for the purpose of announcing something ostensibly newsworthy." The main purposes for which brands utilize press releases are as follows:

- Announce the launch of an event
- Announce a new product, company member, facility, or latest technologies
- Announce an award, achievement, or milestone
- News or updates from social or government organizations

The benefit of a press release is gained exposure in various media outlets, including journalists and social media, and establishing a foothold in search engines. Furthermore, according to the ThomasNet Industrial Purchasing Barometer, it has been found that:

- Seventy-seven percent of industrial buyers say that product news is important to them in their job.

- Seventy percent of buyers look online for new industrial product news.

- Seventy-three percent of buyers would like an easy way to have new industrial product news delivered right to their inbox.

What a Press Release Should Contain

Before composing a press release, consider the following:

- The news should be written specifically for journalists and media. A press release is not an article or a story. If a press release is written as an article, it will most likely be rejected.

- The piece should contain full contact information, such as mailing address and phone number. This will provide credibility for journalists.

- Keep the release short and to the point.

- Leave out promotional or marketing language.

- Select a catchy title or headline.

- The release should not be written in all caps.

- Make sure the release is really newsworthy.

Finally, make use of the following basic tenets of journalism when planning your message:

- Who?
- What?
- When?
- Where?
- Why?
- How?

Press Release Format

Although press releases use different formats from time to time, the following format is generally accepted and should be utilized when appropriate:

- **Title or Headline**. Announces the news; usually under 80 characters

- **Date and Place**. When and where the release originated

- **Introduction**. Answering "Why"

- **Body**. Provides more in-depth information relevant to the news, like statistics or brand background

- **Boilerplate**. A brief "about" section

- **Contact Information**. The name, phone number, email address, mailing address, or other contact information for the PR or other media relations contact person

- **Ending:** ### indicates the end of the press release

There are a wide selection of available templates if you're having difficulty writing a press release. Google Docs is a great source of templates for press releases.

How to Distribute Press Releases

If you have a prior relationship with individuals in the media, like TV journalists, news agencies, or newspaper or magazine writers, you can email them directly with your press releases. If you don't have any media contacts, you can still email people directly if they are in the right field. For example, if you have a press release containing the details of a new car model, you could email blogs or publications that focus on automobiles.

You can also submit a press release to the Associated Press or local publications. Or, you can use one of the following sites: PRWeb, PR Newswire, or PressRelease.com.

1. Analyzing Social Media Platforms

According to an article published through CNBC on January 28, 2014, marketing research firm Demand Metric discovered that roughly two-thirds of organizations — 64 percent of which are claimed as small businesses — use social media analytics. Even more interesting, the research found that three-fourths of the participants in the study reported executive decision-making is influenced through intelligence gathered via social media.

While around 25 to 30 percent of small businesses are not taking advantage of this trend, expect this to change in the immediate future. Social media isn't going away anytime soon, and now is the time for businesses to learn how to properly engage in social media so they can discover what customers (and competitors) are saying and doing about their brand.

2. What Does Social Media Analytics Mean?

Before going any further, an explanation of social media analytics and why they're important to your PR strategy is required. Simply put, social media analytics gathers data from blogs and social media platforms and analyzes it to help you make future business decisions. The most common use of social media analytics is to better understand customer sentiment to improve marketing and customer service activities.

3. Why Analyze?

When it comes to social media, you must establish two things: engagement and community. Social media analytics can allow you to gain insight into social discussions that are directly related to your key focus and help you tap into those conversations to market more effectively. In fact, major companies such as Whirlpool, JetBlue, and the Royal Bank of Canada have used social media analytics to engage customers in response to their feedback. Even Apple has an interest in social media analytics. In December 2013, Apple acquired Topsy Labs, a company that analyzes messages on Twitter.

If you're attempting to track, test, and measure the content you've been sharing on social media to figure out what's working and what isn't according to your fans and followers, consider the following questions:

- What are consumers saying and hearing about my brand?
- What are the most talked about product attributes in my niche? Is the feedback good or bad?
- What is the competition doing to excite the market?
- Is my reputation as an employer affecting my ability to recruit top talent?
- What is the reputation of the new vendors I am considering?
- What issues are a priority for my constituency?

4. What Defines Social Impact?

Social impact is another important element of your brand you must carefully consider when looking to secure PR for your startup. According to Google, there are four different attributes that will define your social impact, which include:

- **Network Referrals.** Understand how visitors from different social sources engage with your site.
- **Conversions.** Measure monetary sales that originally came from social sources.

- **Landing Pages.** Know which pages and content are being shared, as well as where they're being shared and how.
- **Social Plugins.** Allow your users to share content on social networks directly from your site.

How to Analyze

There are countless tools and services, both free and paid, which provide social media analytics information regarding valuable consumer-generated feedback for your brand. The following are several steps you can use to identify and analyze consumer-generated feedback to improve your social media marketing, social impact, and brand awareness:

- **Objectives**. What are you using the data for? Examples include: competitive analysis, product extensions, product strengths and weaknesses, new uses of products, and reactions to advertising and promotions.

- **Identify Keywords**. Finding specific words that bring people to you is a vital step. Besides broader words that describe your business, also search for combinations, product names, or competitors' brand names.

- **Identify Social Media Data Sources**. Not all tools work on all platforms, which is why you need to use the right tools for the right social media platform.

- **Organize Data**. Your data will not be limited to text. Visuals like photos, videos, and artwork are included in your data, which must be organized. Whether you use software or construct your own method of organization, you must compile your data and keep it systematized for analyzing.

- **Analyze Data**. Review your data thoroughly. Begin by understanding the information, and then identify the themes you have observed.

Using Spreadsheets

One of the easiest and most cost effective ways to analyze your social media data is by creating a spreadsheet, usually through Excel or Google Docs. When creating a spreadsheet, you typically want to construct 14 columns that include the following:

- Data
- Network
- Categories
- Subcategories
- Target
- Calls to action
- Meta-tags
- Posts
- Impressions
- Comments (replies)
- Likes (favorites)

- Shares (retweets)
- Clicks
- Total engagement

Fill in the appropriate data you've gathered into the correct column. Once you've entered the data into the spreadsheet, you'll have to sort and analyze your data. By creating a spreadsheet, you can make decisions on how to alter your content strategy.

Because there are different spreadsheets that work better with certain social media platforms, Ann Smarty has outlined spreadsheet examples you can use for social media analytics.

- **GetTweets.** Allows you to export Twitter search results into a spreadsheet.

- **FacebookLikes.** Provides like count, share count, comment count, and overall interaction of your Facebook account.

- **Facebook Fans.** This will fetch the number of Facebook fans engaged with your brand and displays data via a pie chart.

Tools

Analyzing social media can be overwhelming and time consuming. Thankfully, there are a number of tools that can help you collect and understand your data. Here are five examples:

- **Google Analytics**. A comprehensive analytics service, this tool provides you with everything from the number of daily visits to your site, the demographics of your users, how they got to your site, how long visitors stay on your site, and which of your pieces of content are most (and least) popular.

- **Klout**. Utilize Klout to create a map that allows you to visualize all of your social media activity from the last 90 days.

- **HootSuite**. HootSuite's free dashboard allows you to manage all of your social media accounts in one location. However, a paid version features an effective analytics tool.

- **Wildfire**. You can measure your social media performance, receive alerts on trends, and compare your social media base against competitors with this effective tool.

- **Buffer**. This is an app that allows you to manage all of your social media accounts, and features an analytics tool as well.

The Importance of Social Media Monitoring

Social media monitoring can also be called social listening. This is just the process of identifying and assessing what is being said about a company, individual, product, or brand on the Internet; specifically on social media.

Why is this important? Social media monitoring is a great way for you to engage and interact with consumers and potential customers. Through this interaction, you can discover customer behavior. By identifying what supporters (and critics) say about your social media campaign, you can make adjustments and better predict future consumer habits.

There is a wide and varied range of social media monitoring tools available, such as Alerti. This free service allows you to manage and interact with all of your social media accounts from one location. More importantly, the service creates alerts for the keywords of your choice, filters and analyzes information, and measures your social media engagement. Alerti also allows users to collect search results and convert data into graphs, charts, or tasks so you can effectively construct a community around your company or brand.

Social Media Analytics Key Terms

Use case. Utilize this service to analyze a specific scenario.

Project. Cases are configured, reviewed, and analyzed with the project feature.

Source. This is the type of media site from which a document originated.

Snippet. A snippet is a segment of text which is relevant to your analysis.

Concept. This is the topic to search for in social media that is relevant for a specific use case.

Type. Type refers to a group of concepts.

Hotword. A hotword is an aspect which is relevant across several concepts.

Sentiment term. This describes a word or words that express the tone of a sentiment.

Media set. A media set is a group of web addresses that will represent a specific category of a website.

Area of analysis. These are the reports which are organized into three different areas of analysis: Social Media Impact, Segmentation, and Discovery.

Activities to Try

Select three brands on social media and apply analytics. Also, compare and contrast the brands selected with their competitors on social media.

Based on your findings, what worked? What needs altering?

Sources:

http://pic.dhe.ibm.com/infocenter/sma/v1r2m0/index.jsp?topic=%2Fcom.ibm.swg.ba.cognos.ag_ci.1.2.0.doc%2Fcoverview.html

http://www.quirks.com/articles/2013/20131012.aspx

https://support.google.com/analytics/answer/1683971?hl=en

http://www.nytimes.com/2013/12/03/technology/apple-buys-topsy-a-social-media-analytics-firm.html?_r=0

http://customerthink.com/can_you_hear_me_now_top_five_voice_of_customer_pitfalls/

http://www.kmworld.com/Articles/Editorial/Feature/Text-analytics-finds-dynamic-growth-in-e-discovery-and-customer-feedback-76365.aspx

http://www.americanbanker.com/btn/24_6/social-crm-tough-worthy-goal-1038025-1.html

Influencers and Local Social Marketing

There has been an emerging form of marketing within the last decade that's focusing on specific keywords or types of individuals as opposed to the entire target market. Commonly referred to as "influence marketing," it identifies individuals who have influence over potential customers, and dictates marketing activities around these so-called influencers.

Who Are the Influencers?

Influence marketing is defined as "a power affecting a person, thing, or course of events, especially one that operates without any direct or apparent effort." But, who exactly are the people making these decisions? Who are the influencers?

Influencers are everyday people who have the right connections. It's through these connections that these individuals have the "power to affect purchase decisions of others because of their (real or perceived) authority, knowledge, position, or relationship. In_consumer spending, members of a peer group or reference group act as influencers. In business to business (organizational) buying, internal employees (engineers, managers, purchasers) or external consultants act as influencers."

In other words, influencers are people that can drive leads and sales. They're active on social media or blogs. They're brand advocates and niche promoters. They're trendsetters.

Identifying Your Influencers

Now that you know how an influencer can impact your marketing campaign, it's time to look at how you can identify influencers for your specific target market and use them to your advantage.

Besides exploring lists of generic influencers, you can utilize market research techniques that use a pre-defined criteria to determine the extent and type of influence. For example, in the 2003 book, The Influentials, Edward Keller and Jonathan Berry provided the following types of influencers:

- Activists. Influencers who get involved within their communities, political movements, charities, etc.
- Connected. Influencers who have established extensive social networks.
- Impact. Influencers who are looked up to and trusted by others.
- Active minds. Influencers who have multiple and diverse interests.

- Trendsetters. Influencers who are usually early adopters (or leaders) in markets.

Another means of identifying potential influencers comes from consumer or business marketing. Consumer markets involve more emotion, brand loyalty, and word-of-mouth. Business markets are more task-oriented and involve lengthy sales cycles with people who are removed from the purchasing decision: consultants, analysts, journalists, academics, and regulators.

Since some business influencers have more sway than others, a method of ranking these influencers is required. Influencer50 put together the following guidelines:

- **Market Reach**. How many people can an individual connect with?
- **Independence**. Does an influencer have a vested interest in promoting a particular point of view?
- **Frequency of Impact**. How many opportunities does an individual have to influence buying decisions?
- **Expertise.** Is the influencer an expert in the subject matter?
- **Persuasiveness**. Can the influencer change people's minds?
- **Thoroughness of Role**. Can the influencer reach across the decision lifecycle?

Using Online Social Media Tools to Identify Influencers

One of the most effective ways to determine your specific influencers is to use social media tools. These tools can assist you in locating influencers by social listening and by using specific social media marketing metrics. These are only a sample of the tools that can help you determine who your influencers may be:

- **Alianzo.** A community tool that will list and organize blogs, Twitter, and Facebook accounts through an impact/influence algorithm, its focus is mainly in European and Latin America/Spanish speaking sites.

- **Alltop.** This aggregator lists the top blogs in various categories.

- **BlogDash.** This blogger outreach platform will search for indexed bloggers and filters by Scribnia rating, Google Page Rank, and Klout Score. It also provides other metrics, influencer bio, and contact information.

- **CircleCount.** Designed to breakdown Google+, this tool allows you to view a person's bio, profile rank, number of followers, average activity, and links to other social media channels.

- **Commun.it.** A Twitter-based management platform, this will indicate the users that you are connected to. It also helps prioritize influence on your Twitter account and identifies whom you have influence over.

- **Cyfe.** Through a series of built-in widgets, Cyfe monitors everything from Facebook and WordPress to Google Analytics, MailChimp, and Salesforce.

- **eCairn**. This blogger and influencer outreach tool includes a robust collaboration and monitoring features.

- **Empire Avenue**. Featuring a social networking game structure, this connects businesses with individuals on "value relationships."

- **GaggleAMP**. Create so-called "gaggles" with this tool, which are a set of users placed around specific content who receive an alert when new social content goes out. They can then share it within their own networks.

- **Infinigraph**. This is focused on defining the strength of user connections to brands, affinities, and social activities through an algorithm that ranks social connections.

- **Klout**. Measure your ability to move your network to action with this tool.

- **Kred**. Kred is a score-producing, public face similar to Klout.

- **Listorious**. This is a Twitter List indexing site which will organize community-produced Twitter lists into categories.

- **mPact.** This dashboard will show the top 10 influencers by default, along with competitor tracking and contrasting influencers in different categories.

- **Onalytica.** Onalytica is an influencer identification and cursory CRM package located in Great Britain.

- **Peer Index.** This is another Twitter influencer tool.

- **Pulse.** This is an Influencer Program on LinkedIn which allows thought leaders to share their original content directly with LinkedIn users.

- **ReSearch.ly.** Containing search-based filters, this tool can identify mentions of search terms on Twitter.

- **Technorati Authority.** This is the original influence scale. By using Technorati's authority score (the green number associated with a given blog on Technorati.com), you can see the number of unique sites that linked to a given blog in the last six months.

- **Traackr.** A custom topic influencer research tool, Traackr will create a dynamic top-25 list in each category weekly.

- **TweetLevel.** This produces the overall Twitter population list that can be filtered by influence, popularity, engagement, and trust.

- Twitalyzer. This provides a Twitter analysis of network, reach, and impact.

How to Reach Out to Influencers

You've identified your particular influencers, but how can you engage them? While it may seem intimidating, it's not that much different than establishing any other relationship in your life. For example, you can use the following suggestions when reaching out to influencers.

- **Introduce Yourself**. If you're already on a social network, then why not begin by using those resources to introduce yourself? LinkedIn, for example, accomplishes this easily by linking your first-hand connection to influential connections you do not have.

- **Interact**. This is most useful for Twitter, which is perhaps the best tool for first-time interactions with influencers that can affect your audience. Whether you retweet, favorite, or comment on the tweets of influencers, Twitter is an effective and simple way to interact and engage.

- **Ask Questions**. Don't be ashamed to ask a question to an influencer. More than likely, they'll be more than happy to respond.

- **Keep in Touch**. Once you've made an introduction, keep in touch with the influencer so that you won't be forgotten.

- **Remind Them About Upcoming Campaigns**. Inform your influencers when you have an upcoming campaign that you are running. Make sure this doesn't appear too much like spam.

- **Create Lists**. Make a list of the most popular influencers in your niche and share it with your audience. A top 10 will suffice. This will give influencers more of an incentive to interact with you.

- **Listen**. Pay attention to what your influencers are saying. If they promote content relevant to your business, thank them for sharing and share it yourself. If you notice they are talking about something in their personal lives, like a favorite TV show or if they're having a bad day, make a comment. They will remember.

Local Social Marketing

Narrowing down your search for local influencers is equally as important as establishing connections with influencers across the world. In fact, local social marketing is the next big thing.

For example, there have been over 2 billion unique Local searches per month on Google from Desktop computers in the United States. Furthermore, over 50 percent of mobile queries have local intent. Since more and more users are using smartphones, local marketing is of the utmost importance.

There are various types of local search sites. These include:

- **Search Engine Maps**. Google, Bing, and Yahoo
- **Review Sites**. Yelp, Urban Spoon, Zagat
- **Yellow Page Directories**. Insider Pages, Superpages
- **Local Directories**. CitySearch, Localeze
- **Business Directories**. InfoGroup/InfoUSA, Acxiom
- **Niche, Industry Specific Directories.** Health Grades

Principles of Local Social Marketing

The following key elements should be included in local social marketing for optimized engagement:

- Claim and verify local listings
- Manage listings for multiple locations
- Optimize local listings for increased local SEO traffic
- Eliminate duplicate listings
- Increase and manage reviews
- Submit your business to additional local directories
- Setup analytics tracking to properly track local activity
- Promote your local listings

Local Social Marketing Tools

Every social media format has a search function that can be refined to local businesses. There are also apps like FourSquare and Meetup where people can meet at a location based on who is nearby or common interests. FourSquare, for example, will offer incentives for frequent visitors. You can also review the chapter on social monitoring tools to discover what people are saying about you or your brand.

Other tools for local social marketing include:

- **Google AdWords Keyword Tool**. This is the most popular SEO tool that can be used as a location marker in your initial keyword list.

- **Whitespark's Local Citation Finder**. Since citations are "the life juice" of local SEO, you'll need a citation finder. This app creates your own online citations and receives new citation ideas for your business.

- **GetListed**. You can use this tool to see if you're included on popular local business websites, including YellowPages, CitySearch, Yelp, and Localeze.

- **Instamonial by KnexxLocal**. This free app helps spread word-of-mouth by sharing your brand within all of your social media channels.

Events

Having a lauch event, running regular promotions, or being part of other organizational events can be an important part of your PR.

How Social Media Can Help Promote an Event

By now, you should understand the importance of social media in public relations. But, how can you actually use social media to promote an event?

You Can Easily Organize an Event

- **Collaborate.** You have the ability to work with other event organizers, which can save everyone involved some extra time and effort.

- **Collect RSVP's Online.** Using specific tools, you can gather your RSVP's in one location and keep these attendees up-to-date on the event.

- **Engagement.** Involve potential attendees by asking or polling them on what they would like to see at the event.

- **Find Suppliers.** 61 percent of customers read an online review before making a purchase. When planning your event, use online reviews to find venues, caterers, photographers, etc.

Promote the Event

- **Create Event Listings.** Spread the word on every social network. For example, you can create an event on Facebook or LinkedIn for free.

- **Integration.** Since 71 percent of users will purchase a product if it was referred to them on social media, have people who registered for your event share it with their social network.

- **Use Hashtags.** The inclusion of hashtags makes it easier for people to locate and share your event.

- **Promotional Videos.** Creating a video can generate buzz and anticipation for your event. In fact, 76 percent of marketers have claimed that video marketing is going to be a top priority.

Encourage Engagement

- **Offer Prizes.** Awarding a prize to the most engaged attendees is another way to create excitement and continued engagement.

- **Live-stream the Event.** Not everyone can make the event, so show them what they're missing while also reaching a global audience.

- **Live Twitter Feed.** Keep the excitement going by live tweeting the event. Since hashtags receive twice as much engagement as those that don't, this is a simple tactic to encourage more followers.

- **Encourage Check-ins at Different Locations.** There is always the chance that people will miss certain booths or attractions, so offering an incentive for people to check-in at different locations gives others the chance to see more of the event.

- **Offer Customer Support:** Make sure you have customer support to help attendees with any questions they have, such as directions or schedule of events.

Extend the Event

- **Upload Highlights to YouTube.** Give attendees the opportunity to remember the event with video highlights, as well as encourage others to attend in the future.

- **Share Presentations/Write Blog Posts.** Share your experiences and discoveries of your event by creating either a presentation or blog post. This will also generate buzz for the event, even if it already took place.

- **Share Photos.** Collect photos and highlight all of your hard work on Pinterest or Instagram.

- **Get Feedback.** By gathering feedback, you'll better understand what attendees liked and didn't like about the event. You can use this information for future events, and it maintains the conversation between you and your fans.

- **Keep Your Online Community Engaged.** You may not be able to physically host an event that frequently, but you still want to keep your online community engaged year round. Hold weekly webinars and chats or engage them through daily social media discussions.

Tools For Event Planning

There are an abundance of websites and smartphone apps that can assist you in planning an event. Whether that involves creating and sending out invitations or local search apps, planning an event has never been so simple and convenient. You can use any of the following tools:

- **Acteva**. Acteva is an online ticketing, registration, and payment management system for both online and real-life events.

- **Anyvite**. As a basic invite site that can be viewed across multiple platforms, Anyvite includes excellent mobile functionality.

- **Circle**. This app that lets you see when your friends and connections are in the same area.

- **Ejovo**. On top of online invitation, Ejovo offers everything from party themes, décor, and recipes.

- **Eventbrite**. This allows you to create events, sell tickets, track registrations, and manage your event entries.

- **Evite**. Designs for invitations and party ideas abound with evite, which is mainly for kid's events or informal parties.

- **Facebook Events**. You can create an event, invite, track, and message all of your guests in the largest social network.

- **Foursquare.** Foursquare lets you share and coordinate locations with friends, family, colleagues, or event attendees.

- **Google+ Events.** Use this tool to send personalized invitations through Google+.

- **Joinin.** Joinin helps you create events and chat with people with shared interests.

- **Netvibes.com.** Deliver brand observation rooms and user-personalized marketing campaigns with Netvibes.

- **Pingg.** Pingg allows you to collect both snail mail and online RSVP's via social media or email.

- **Pitchengine.** This tool assists in creating content that you can use for the newsroom, campaign, or event hub, and even your own website or blog.

- **Twtvite.** Create an invite, post to Twitter (complete with hashtags), and track responses with this tool.

- **Ustream.** Ustream gives you the opportunity to broadcast your event.

Chapter Nine: Conclusion

Although it started as a way for businesses to glean editorial mentions and media coverage, public relations has taken a new form with the help of the Internet.

Nowadays, PR is no longer about purely gaining exposure for your business, but also about the following:

- Building relationships with your target audience and industry influencers.
- Creating a compelling story about your brand.
- Maintaining a relationship with your PR network.

PR is important for businesses, and especially for startups, because it allows them to create brand awareness, establish their credibility within the industry, and build trust among their target market. As a result, it's much easier for companies to promote their products and services — and convince their customers to buy or subscribe.

But to kick off your campaign, you will need to create and share your brand's story. This gives your company a face, therefore making it human. It's easier to tickle your audience's senses and encourage them to take favorable action in this way.

However, this process requires an effective PR strategy that includes the following:

- Defining your campaign objectives.
- Creating your business' key message.
- Choosing which platform to bring out your message to the public.
- Building a network of PR professionals and industry influencers who can help promote your brand.
- Finding the right key metrics to measure your campaign's success.

To put it simply, an effective PR strategy is imperative to properly execute your campaign and generate desired results for your startup business.

In the era where the market is saturated with an array of companies, products, and services, PR is one of the best ways to gain exposure for your startup. But more than bringing your brand to the spotlight, it's used to establish your reputation and your business' place within the market. Hence, it's very important that you identify the PR professionals and industry influencers who can support the products and services you offer to achieve your business' PR marketing campaign.

The key is to create something newsworthy and find the right partners to distribute and syndicate content for ultimate exposure. Your success will largely depend on your ability to create newsworthy content, come up with fresh pitches, appropriately contact the press, build relationships, and leverage those relationships for optimal results.

Chapter Ten:

Resources

Online Guides

- Introduction to Public Relations
  Whether you would like to start a career as a PR professional or craft a PR campaign for your startup, this guide by ipr.gov.uk provides you with the information you will need about public relations. From tools and techniques, the disciplines of the industry, and choosing the right PR firm or specialist, this guide will help you get through the ropes of public relations.

- The Beginner's Guide to PR by Publicize
  This guide by Publicize is ideal for people who are new to PR; especially those who would like to get PR for their startup. The selling point of this guide is the *PR for SEO* chapter, which explains how public relations can boost a company's organic search rankings.

- The Beginner's Guide to Online Marketing: Get the Word Out with PR by Neil Patel and Ritika Puri
  If you prefer visual content, this infographic created by Neil Patel and Ritika Puri about public relations is what

you need. What's great about this guide is that it provides a list of tools and services you can use to automate and streamline your PR process.

Blog Posts

- Creative Content is Your Best Public Relations Outreach by Rebecca Corliss
  With people buying stories instead of products or services nowadays, there is no denying that your startup needs creative content to gain exposure. This post by Rebecca Corliss on HubSpot informs that you do not need a fancy PR campaign to get publicity.

- Developing a PR Plan by Rachel Meranus
  It was mentioned again and again in this book that a PR campaign would not work without an effective plan. If you are looking for tips to create a PR campaign strategy for your startup, this post by Rachel Meranus on Entrepreneur will assist you.

- Pro Tips for Finding Your PR Specialty by Alex Honeysett
  Whether you are looking for a job as a PR specialist or launching your own PR consultancy, Alex Honeysett's post on The Muse will teach you the first steps on finding your specialty within the public relations industry.

Websites

- PR Daily

  PR Daily is a daily news site that delivers news, advice, and opinions on public relations, marketing, social media, and media works.

- Cutting Edge PR

  Conceptualized by Kim Harrison of Century Consulting, this website allows you to read free articles about key areas of public relations such as planning, ethics, and communication management.

- Public Relations Society of America

  PRSA is a community of PR and communications professionals across the United States. They provide training and professional development to PR pros, allowing them to boost their career on public relations. Their website also provides information about upcoming PR webinars, events, and the latest job bulletins.

State of Public Relations 2014:
http://www.slideshare.net/Vocus/state-of-public-relations-2014

Ria Von Enterprises: http://riavonenterprises.com/content-is-the-single-most-important-part-of-your-successful-website/

Publicize: http://www.publicize.co/beginners-guide-to-pr/

Chapter Eleven:

PR People to Follow on Twitter

Public relations would not be an important practice if not for the help of PR professionals. They exist to help businesses tell important stories about their brand. These PR pros are worth knowing, not only because of the company they represent, but for what they have contributed to the industry.

Ten PR people you should follow on Twitter are:

1. **Bill Stoller**
   With 25 years of experience as a PR professional, Bill helps businesses get their share of publicity and social media. He is the founder of Free Publicity, "the newsletter for PR-hungry businesses!" Follow him on Twitter: @PublicityGuru

2. **Danny Brown**
   Danny blogs about marketing and social media and what these two things mean to us humans. His blog is recognized as the no. 1 marketing blog in the world by HubSpot and was included in Social Media Examiner's Top 10 Social Media Blogs in 2011, 2013, and 2014. Follow him on Twitter: @DannyBrown

3. **David Meerman Scott**

   David in an online marketing strategist and author of several books on marketing, with *The New Rules of Marketing and PR* as his most notable published work. The book sold over 250,000 copies and was printed in more than 25 languages. Follow him on Twitter: @dmscott

4. **Paul Hartunian**

   Paul is a world-renowned free publicity expert. He is also known as the New Jersey man who sold the Brooklyn Bridge. Follow him on Twitter: @paulhartunian

5. **Deirdre Breakenridge**

   A veteran in PR and marketing and author of five Financial Times books, Dreidre is the CEO of Pure Performance Communications — a company that takes advantage of creative communication to foster deeper engagement and build stronger relationships. Her latest published work is *Social Media and Public Relations: Eight New Practices for the PR Professional*. Follow her on Twitter: @dbreakenridge

6. **Dorothy Crenshaw**

   Dorothy is the founder of Dorothy Crenshaw, her namesake agency that provides ongoing PR consultation. She speaks frequently on brand-building, marketing to women, and workplace topics, and was named by PR Week as one of the industry's 100 Most Powerful Women. Follow her on Twitter: @dorocren

7. **Mary Lower**

   Using high tech tools to share traditional tales, Mary does PR, media relations, and social media for Sterling Cross Group. In 2012, she won the Established Woman Award at the National Association of Women Business Owners – Minneapolis chapter. Follow her on Twitter: @PRMoxie

8. **Alan Weinkratz**

   Alan has 30 years of experience in tech PR, working on new technologies and standards to help advance a business' vision and story to the media, industry analysts, thought leaders, and bloggers. He helps startups become successful content producers through Social Internet. Follow him on Twitter: @alanweinkratz

9. **Brian Solis**

   As a digital analyst, Brian studies the effects of disruptive technology on business and society. He is also one of the most prominent thought leaders in digital transformation. His latest book, *What's the Future of Business*, explores how business and customer relationships unfold in four distinct moments of truth. Follow him on Twitter: @briansolis

10. **Dave Fleet**

    A well-known figure in the Canadian social media environment, Dave is currently the Senior Vice President of Digital in Edelman's Toronto office. He is responsible for developing and implementing digital engagement strategies for some of the world's best-known brands across consumer, corporate, technology, and public affairs verticals. Follow him on Twitter: @davefleet

Chapter Twelve:
Tips by the Experts

"There is both an insatiable demand for content on sites like our's but also a seemingly endless supply," said Peter Page, associate editor at Entrepreneur.com. *"I tell would-be contributors to read the site thoroughly to get the sense of what we publish and then tailor submissions for us. We are patient with people who make the effort. We don't pay contributors but we give priceless exposure. It is up to the contributors to use publication here to meet their larger goals."*

Peter Page, assistant editor, Entrepreneur.com

- *Brief beats long.*
- *Relevant beats not-relevant: be familiar with the outlet you're pitching to.*
- *Access to top executives—especially prominent ones—goes really far in helping to sell a story.*

Jon Fine, Executive Editor, Inc. Magazine

"You're new and no one has ever heard of you. Tough spot. But getting noticed doesn't need to be as hard as you might think. In fact, it happens every single day. Partnerships. That's a key word here. Think "celebrity". Yes, it's tough to ask a noted name to endorse you, but with a bit of

homework, you can greatly increase your chances for success. First, understand the qualities and features of your product or service that truly make it stand out from the competition. If you can't point to one or two things that make your product a head-and-shoulders stand out, back to the drawing board.

But with that info in hand, you can begin researching which big names have ideals, philosophies and histories that align with your product's features. Approaching them with a winner you know they're going to like will be a big step forward. That, and plan for some money, too. Paying for their support is a given, but getting their attention will come down to how well you impress them in the first place.

From that moment forward, it'll matter less who you are and more who your friends are. Their reach will get you started and you can build from that success."

Duane Forrester, Sr. Product Manager, Webmaster Outreach at Bing

"If you're trying to build buzz for your startup, you either need to build some strong relationships with industry leaders and journalists or you need to nurture the ones that you already have.

What I like to do is to find all of the relevant journalists that cover your particular niche, you can do that with the Cision tool, Muck Rack, Get Little Bird and a couple others, but the key is to find the most influential people writing about your space.

Next, I then add those folks to a private Twitter list. Once that list is created, I monitor it daily and find interesting tweets from these influencers to engage with. You want to build relationships with these influencers and sharing and interacting with their content is a way get their attention.

You have to ease into relationships with these influencers... You don't meet them and immediately ask for a favor, just like you don't meet a potential girlfriend/boyfriend and immediately jump into bed with them. You must nurture the relationships. Like their posts, favorite their tweets, retweet them, share their content and comment on their blogs. This is a great way to build trust with that influencer and actually get them to want to do something for you.

Pitching PR to influencers is different that traditional PR. As the Tech Tools for Entrepreneurs columnist for Inc. Magazine, I get pitched stuff all of the time. And if you ask for a favor before even being friendly, your chances of me writing about you decrease substantially.

Personally, I need to demo the tool, try it out, see where the value of the tool is and get comfortable with it before I can honestly recommend it to tens of thousands of people.

Get to know the people you are pitching. Or bring on a consultant who already has these relationships to help you rock your startup."

Travis Wright - Chief Marketing Technologist CCP Global, Inc. Magazine Columnist & Venture Catalyst

"Editors get bombarded with emails on a consistent basis. For tech startups in particular this is a drawback, not least because when their emailed press release hits an editor's inbox the press release comes from an unnamed brand and is usually covered in tech speak. Result? The delete button.

The solution to this is to pick up the phone and speak to the editor in person. Editors rarely get phoned anymore which makes them far more open to hearing a real life person's voice on the other end of the phone. Speak to them as you would a friend, informally and with no pretence, and tell them a little bit about your new launch. You'd be surprised how well this strategy works"

Jez Walters, Editor, What's New in Publishing.

"One of the best ways to get PR for your startup is to generate stellar content. However, one mistake made by a lot of new entrepreneurs is that the content they create is too much centered on the product or service surrounding their venture. Instead, you should focus on displaying your industry expertise and impart that to your readers and social media followers. Better yet, take an interesting stance on a particular issue in your niche and back it up with a factual argument. It's implicit that your ultimate goal is to generate revenues and profits when garnering PR for your startup – don't make that the overriding theme of your content."

Andrew Schrage (Money Crashers)

"Talk to the editor on the phone. They get bombarded with emails so you're more likely to get through over the phone. Getting a two-way conversation started is really important – ask the edtior questions to get them going. After all, they are a journalist – they love talking about themselves! Be sure to show interest in them – they will often be flattered if you reference their latest post.

Smiling on the phone is really important – you sound clearer when talking this way. Walking around instead of sitting down whilst you're on the phone works for some people too.

Have facts written out in bullet points in front of you when talking over the phone – "I'll send over the top line stat." Should they ask any questions over the phone, note them down to improve your next pitch."

Barrie Smith, Marketing Consultant, Receptional.

"Most startups will write press releases and send them to named journalists at selected titles or they will use a generic press release newswire service such as UBM's PR Newswire. This is a well-worn strategy. What is perhaps less well known, however, is that press release newswires carry a lot of SEO clout not just for your company name but also your product and services.

My tip is therefore to insert keywords into your press releases that adequately describe your product and services, as well as links back to relevant pages on your website. By doing this consistently, over a period of months, you should be pleasantly surprised at how PR works for you, not just in terms of awareness but also in terms of organic search for your startup."

Alex Attinger, Group MD, digitalbox.com

"You will need to reach relevant people in the press to get the word out about your startup. It can be difficult to get through to the bigger names in the press, so go after bloggers at first. Not only can you find lots of bloggers for most any niche, but also they're typically passionate about the topic and they have influence within the sector you're trying to penetrate. Try Alltop, Buzzsumo, and Google blog search to identify bloggers, and create a spreadsheet of bloggers, urls of their posts, and notes about them. Then start contacting them to pitch yourself."

Shawn Collins, Co-Founder, Affiliate Summit

"Sustained brand building through effective PR is essential to start-up success. If you stand if front of your office location with a bullhorn and announce you are "open for business" and "taking new customers" few people will listen and nobody will take action. However, if you read this book and learn how to constantly and relentlessly leverage PR opportunities to share valuable content, tell interesting stories, and from

time to time indirectly promote your stuff you will increase your likelihood of start-up success exponentially. This priceless book by Murray Newlands and Drew Hendricks is your pain pill to an otherwise ineffective PR strategy."

Kristopher Jones, Founder of LSEO.com and KBJ Capital

"The bloggers and journalists you'll be reaching out to aren't fools - they know you want something from them. And that's OK. They want something from you, too: A good story to tell. They want something new, something different and something other people don't have.

Of course, you can't give everyone an exclusive, but choose a small handful of writers at a small handful of sites you're really interested in getting publicity in. Know what those writers cover. Craft your pitch to them in a way that appeals to their interests and their coverage area. Get to know them before you need them. Do your research and find out which reporters are the ones you'll want to reach out to.

Do not - repeat, do not - just send out press releases to the general tips email of a publication. They get hundreds, if not thousands, of pitches there and the chance of getting your email read are slim. The chance that your press release will be interesting enough to spark their interest is even slimmer.

When you reach out to the blogger or journalist, tell them why they care. And ask that if they are not interested, if they could suggest someone else you could reach out to at their publication. Don't ask them to pass it along; just ask for the suggestion of who that should be.

Above all, don't take rejection personally. Just because this person isn't writing about you now doesn't mean he or she won't in the future. In fact, if you smile and thank them anyway, there's a better chance that next time around they'll at least hear you out, because you weren't a jerk."

Amy Vernon, Chief cook and bottle-washer, Amy Vernon, LLC

"It's all about relationships. If you spent your first year doing nothing but building relationships through attending networking events, listening, following up, having lunches, listening, following up, reading and consuming other people's work, and following up, you would have accomplished a task that many PR professionals don't accomplish in their entire career. Have a system, ideally a CRM (customer relationship management) tool, to manage this flood of relations and maintain copious notes on how you met and what you heard. In a very short time it'll be the most valuable tool in your PR arsenal."

David Spark (@dspark), Founder, Spark Media Solutions

"Startups need to develop a positive reputation quickly. In the online wold of today, reputation has less to do with word-of-mouth and more to do with the nationwide reputation of a business. Instead of waiting for this to happen organically, a smart start up will start the process of creating a positivereputation through publicity of various types."

Brian Horn, Co-Founder Authority Alchemy

"If you plan on pitching me and I don't know your name… you won't get a response. Follow me and be part of my community before pitching me your business."

John Rampton, Entrepreneur, writer for Forbes, Entrepreneur.com, Inc, Huffington Post and many more.

"Your private messages aren't always private; If you can't tweet it, don't write it in an email or text it. Your "private" messages can be forwarded, captured in screenshots and published in blogs, putting you and/or your brand at risk for public relations issues than can go viral in social media and cause irreversible damage in search results. This is not the potential top tier media coverage a start-up or any company strives for, but the consequences of a pissy email to a co-worker or sexting message can land you in the wrong limelight."

@LisaBuyer Author of Social PR Secrets

www.ingramcontent.com/pod-product-compliance
Lightning Source LLC
Chambersburg PA
CBHW051708170526
45167CB00002B/589